HOW

TO *Really* BE A

MOTHER

About the Author

Emily Hourican is a journalist and editor. She writes regularly for the *Sunday Independent* and *Image* magazine and contributes to *Conde Nast Traveller* and *Woman & Home* in the UK. She is editor of *Hospitality Ireland* and she was founding editor of *The Dubliner* magazine. She has three children and lives in Dublin.

HOW *Really* TO BE A MOTHER

EMILY HOURICAN

Gill & Macmillan

Gill & Macmillan
Hume Avenue, Park West, Dublin 12
with associated companies throughout the world
www.gillmacmillanbooks.ie

© Emily Hourican 2013
978 07171 5848 5

Design and print origination by Carole Lynch
Printed and bound by ScandBook AB, Sweden

This book is typeset in Adobe Garamond 11pt on 15pt.

The paper used in this book comes from the wood pulp
of managed forests. For every tree felled, at least one tree is planted,
thereby renewing natural resources.

A CIP catalogue record for this book is available
from the British Library.

1 3 5 4 2

For Malachy, Davy and little B, whose goodwill made this book nearly impossible. And for David.

CONTENTS

Part III: After Birth

ACKNOWLEDGEMENTS

Thank you to all the many people who inspired and informed me, directly and indirectly, beginning with my own mother, Patricia, and my much-missed mother-in-law, Pauline. Thanks to Brendan O'Connor, Cilian Fennell, Trevor White, Ed Brophy and Tom McGurk, all of who have, at one stage or another, suggested I write this book. Some of them even said it twice. To Nicki Howard for really refining the concept and to Kristin Jensen, Deirdre Rennison Kunz and all at Gill & Macmillan, for their great help during the process. Thanks to my friends at the *Sunday Independent,* Anne Harris, Mary O'Sullivan and Madeleine Keane; mothers and mentors. And at *Image* Magazine, thanks to Melanie Morris, Meg Walker, Fran Power and Richard Power. Thanks to my sisters: Bridget, who has wisdom beyond her years, and Martha, who has never-ending faith. To my sisters-in-law Aisling Mulvaney, Fionnghuala Garvie and Paula Gilpin, who have been the constant sounding boards for so much of this. To my agent Jonathan Williams, for his belief and meticulous reading. To Mark and Kevin Kelly, for their support over many years. To Cristina, Leanora and Leah Frawley and Ger McEvilly. To all my friends, but especially, in no order but with much love, Cliona Hannon, Sarah Caden, Sarah Murray, Susan Jane White, Róisín Ingle (for Mothershould), Natasha Fennell, Sinead and Orla Hyland, Rebecca and Sarah O'Donnell, Tara Murphy, Laragh Stuart,

Domini and Peaches Kemp, Grainne Callaghan, Briony Widdis, Joanne Murphy, Jane Babb, Beibhinn Byrne, Emma Kelly, Daire Higgins, Karen Holmes, Karen McCauley, Aoife Doris, Sharin, Rioghnach and Bebhinn Murphy, Sarah McDonnell, Shauna Brown, Eliza Pakenham and Emer Bowman. To the mothers at the school gates, who are kindred spirits and a godsend, Georgina O'Regan, Elaine Quinn, Orlaith Hanrahan, Audrey Buckley, Sam Keyes, Annabelle Tonge, Emer Kennedy, Lorna Brady, Mary Byrne, Mary Thompson, Maureen Curran, Louise Lucas and Viv McKechnie. And to my father, Liam, always.

FROM GENESIS TO REVELATION

Once upon a time, I went to parties full of a desire to scintillate, exchange gossip, meet interesting people, get drunk and come home at dawn. Those were fun times.

Then one night I went to a party and told everyone that I was pregnant. It was the right time to do so. I had reached the three-month mark, was starting to 'show' (something that made me equally proud and horrified) and most of my friends had guessed anyway.

Cue lots of excited hugs and congratulations. Then a hand reached out to my belly. It belonged to a woman I barely knew. Without so much as a by-your-leave, she leaned in and gave me the fullest, most experienced stomach-grope that I have ever received from a non-qualified medical practitioner. Her fingers practically twined around my kidneys.

Simultaneously, two women began to talk over me about their pregnancies and what they had felt/craved/developed. Someone else asked when I was due and instantly followed up with questions about whether I had a changing table, nappy sanitiser, cot, yadda yadda yadda, before telling me that what I *really* needed was… At that point, I switched off.

Within the space of just a few minutes, I had been manhandled, ignored, talked over and lectured.

Perfect.

Right there was all the training and experience I needed for being a mother.

Except that I didn't know it.

I still rashly believed that my life would continue as normal. That *I* would continue as normal, only with a small, adorable child at my side. It has taken me ten years to fully recognise the things that happen to us when we become mothers. Some we do ourselves, some the children are responsible for, and some Society imposes on us. Actually, reverse that – *most* Society imposes on us, some happen naturally and some we complicate our own lives with.

I am not a childcare expert or a 'guru', but I am a mother – of two boys, aged ten and six, and a three-year-old girl – and fascinated by everything to do with children. This means I have had a ringside seat for nearly ten years of the particular type of mess that is modern motherhood. I have lived it, discussed it, reflected on it, read up on it and torn my hair out over it. And my conclusion is that any preparation for motherhood that we are encouraged to make is totally inadequate.

To my astonishment, the reality of having children turned out to be quite, quite different to what I had expected. Everyone goes on about how tired you will be, but they don't often mention the isolation, boredom, insecurity, guilt and fear that come with the more expected stuff, like overwhelming love and joy.

I was pretty familiar with the mechanics of small babies, thanks to my own crazy childhood – second eldest of six, brought up in a bizarre world of expatriate insularity. There were always little ones to be changed, dressed, wiped, read to, saved from falling, fed and walked. But I was only a foot soldier in this, following orders. I wasn't the general. There was no danger I would be court-martialled if things didn't go right. The realities of life at the top of the responsibility hierarchy took me completely by surprise.

So, How To Be A Mother. For most of us, that statement actually needs a question mark. *How* to be a mother? How to *really* be a mother?

How on earth can we switch from career-busting Mistress Of The Universe, or even just average-but-perfectly-happy Career Girl, to Mother in one earth-shattering moment? What bit of being a whizz at spreadsheets and job interviews is going to carry over and be of benefit in our new lives? And how can we reconcile the old and new Us into a happy, uniform whole?

There is no greater reality check than a baby. No matter how fabulous or dynamic you think you are, how expert in diplomacy, beguilement or client pitches, a baby will crash through all of it. You can't fool a baby, flatter it, tell it half the truth, dazzle it with science, charm it or bamboozle it. If you are not funny, a baby will let you know. A baby is not interested in projections of you. It wants what it wants, and if you don't provide, it will yell.

It's Not Just Juggling, It's an Entire Circus Act

This isn't just about fitting into your pre-pregnancy jeans and needing a good night's sleep. It goes deeper than that. This is about the dislocation that occurs after having a baby. The way you go from You to something Other, even when you know that You are still in there somewhere. The way it is all more boring, difficult and unrewarding than you expected, but you don't dare say this to the other mothers you meet in the playground or at coffee mornings. Instead, you smile and coo about how lovely it all is and how you're *simply dreading* going back to work. This book shares the secrets you might mutter to a very close friend, admitting just how inadequate the whole thing makes you feel, but you will always finish with 'of course it's wonderful really and I know I'm very lucky…'

You say this to reassure her, and convince yourself.

This is not a calm look at the issues surrounding motherhood. It's the account of someone living through it, someone who is often frustrated, uncertain and insecure. There are few definite answers and a lot of admissions.

There is also plenty of irritation that motherhood in the modern world should be so intensely pressurised – 'get it right or your kids will suffer for ever' (cue manic, witch-like laughter) – at the very same time as economic and commercial forces are making it almost impossible to do much more than fight fires.

Like the old days of the Circus Maximus, mothers have been fitted out into different archetypes – Routine Mother, Working Mother, Attachment Mother – all with their particular accessories and foibles, thrown into the arena and pitted against one another. Simultaneously, we have been sold a rubbish notion of what motherhood *should* look and feel like, transmitted via endless pretty pictures of an ideal domestic life. We're too busy turning on one other and fighting it out over what age to wean and what degree of separation is acceptable, as well as agonising over our own perceived failures, to confront the fact that Society is busily destroying motherhood.

That was the revelation that came to me somewhere between Baby Number Two and Baby Number Three. It's not that we mothers are bad at what we do, it's that Society likes to make us think we are by holding up a distorting mirror to our lives, a mirror in which nothing we do can ever be good enough.

Some women are naturally incredibly good at motherhood; they don't feel the outside pressures of what to do and be. But for most of us, having children is hard in ways we didn't expect. Here we are, looking over our shoulders, reading childcare books and comparing ourselves with our peers, convinced that there's a trick we have missed or that someone else is doing it better. But you know what? There is no trick and very few of us get it completely right, just as very few of us get it completely wrong. That middle ground is huge; it's where most of us operate, and it's fine. If we all relaxed a bit more, expected a bit less and refused to go head to head with one another, wouldn't we find life easier? And then maybe we would be a little bit better than 'good enough'.

This book contains the kinds of thing your mother might have told you, except that none of our mothers coped with quite as much as we do. Mostly, they didn't work outside the home. Some even had help within the home. Certainly no one expected them to look fabulous, raise geniuses and choose between chess club and Mandarin Chinese, all while absorbing endlessly changing inform-ation about nutritious food and how everything that happens to our children is directly attributable to us mothers.

This is a book to take the sting out of motherhood – all those times when you feel at the end of your tether and your wits, when the delicate balance you've contrived starts to tip into chaos and despair, when you feel like you're getting it wrong while the rest of the world gets it right and worry that your children will suffer the consequences.

And it's for the few times when you feel you've got everything right – family healthy and well fed, laundry done, house tidy, educational but fun games played, quality intimate time spent with your partner – only to find a new feeling struggling inside you, a tiny voice that whispers, 'Is this it?'

This book will set you right, because this one tells the simple truth – that we are all the same, really. We all feel like this, which means that 'this' is normal. And just as we all go into it, we all come through it, emerging stronger and more confident at the end. We learn to recognise what are real concerns and what are silly notions given to us by the world at large – prescriptive nonsense about how we *should* be handling our roles as mothers. This book will speed up that process.

Yes, parenting is a blood sport, and yes, it's the most important thing any of us will do, but that doesn't mean it isn't also hilarious and absurd – something to be laughed at, mocked, pointed at, turned into funny anecdotes and passed around. This is also a book to give a laugh about it all.

It is possible you don't quite know how you got here (I don't mean the birds-and-the-bees bit; it's the psychological bit I'm talking about), but you are, I hope, about to discover that this doesn't matter. Tracking your progress is much less important than enjoying the journey. Grab a glass of wine or an herbal tea and drag your eyes away from the baby monitor (if you're actually clutching it, now is a good moment to gently put it down). Let's take our first steps together.

But just before we do, I should say that if I start trying to count the ways in which I love my children, we will all be here forever. I love every scrap, every bit, every sound of them. I love the way they smell, the things they say. I love the way they have put a rocket under my world and blown it sky high, and the way they have watched, with me, as it re-forms into something much more interesting. They have, each of them, exponentially increased my enjoyment of life. Every time I mention being frustrated, annoyed or challenged in this book, that is only the surface. Underneath it, unchangeable, is the enormous love I feel for them.

Now, we can really begin.

PART I
BIRTH

Chapter 1

THE BIG BANG

In which I have a baby and They actually let me take him home

I went into labour at around midday. That seemed like a good time to invite my sister round for lunch. An hour later, in between emitting the screams of a pig having slices of bacon removed while still alive, I had to ask her to leave. Between howls of pain, I was deeply apologetic at my failure of hospitality.

Once the baby was born, my mother came to stay. Her arrival was like the cavalry. She stayed a week, then when all seemed quiet on the battlefront, went to visit her mother down the country. She had only been gone a few hours when the baby began to howl and wouldn't stop. My husband adopted the long-suffering stance he was to maintain for the next year – patiently walking the floor, screaming child over his shoulder. Up and down. Up and down.

'What's wrong with him?' I asked my sister in panic. In my mother's absence, she was keeping the supportive female commune going.

'Maybe he's hungry.'

'I just fed him.'

'Feed him again?'

I fed him again. He still wouldn't stop crying.

'Do you think he's sick?'

'Where's Mummy? She never should have left us,' my sister said angrily.

On my face, I'm pretty certain, was a certain look that I have since become used to seeing on new mothers. It's not just the black circles under the eyes – you would expect those. It's the stunned, rabbit-in-the-headlights stare; equal parts confusion, fear and exhaustion, mixed with a daze of delight.

I remember it well. To my astonishment, after nine months of expectation and abstract anticipation, The Miracle came to pass. I had a baby. And I found that I wasn't remotely ready. The part of me that wasn't in a dizzy dream of love badly wanted to say to anyone who would listen, 'Look, that's all very well, but actually, I've just realised that I'm not really quite up for this yet. I couldn't even get the car seat into the car at the hospital. Now that I better understand the terms and conditions of this pregnancy thing, could you just take the baby away for another few months while I get my head around it properly, then bring him back and I'll be ready to go?'

What really took me by surprise, you see, was that the baby was a baby. He wasn't a doll, or a toy. He didn't belong to anyone else – I couldn't realistically expect to hand him back to the rightful mother after a few hours. He was mine, to keep. And They (midwives, doctors, people employed to keep society safe) were letting me go home with him, just like that. They hadn't even seen my home. How could They know it was suitable for a baby?

In fact, it wasn't. He was two weeks early, and everyone had told me that first babies are *always* late, so I didn't have anything ready for him. Not even a babygro. Luckily, my wonderful mother-in-law had a few in the attic so she brought them to the hospital, along with a borrowed car seat and far more confidence about holding him than I had.

That feeling – of being caught on the hop, on the back foot – never quite left me. For the next two years, I felt I was somehow playing catch-up, that I wasn't getting it right, that there was a trick I was missing. So I faked it. That's what we all do when confronted with new, challenging situations, right? We put our best foot forward, adopt a confident tone and brazen it out. This fakery never fools the baby, of course. My son could tell that his parents were rank amateurs from the very first second.

Sometimes we dissolve in a heap of snot and tears (in my experience, this happens on Day Three, after nine weeks and the first time you cut their fingernails, because somehow, no matter how careful you are, you nearly always manage to nick the skin and draw a tiny bead of blood. Seeing your baby's blood on the *outside*, not inside where it's supposed to be, is one of the all-time unpleasant feelings). But after a short weep, we pick ourselves up and carry on. Becoming a mother means taking on some of the attributes of the Foreign Legion.

Richard Scarry's Great Big Maternity Book

Doing full justice to all of the many strange, overwhelming and wonderful things that happen when you give birth to a baby, especially if it's your first baby, requires one of those great big activity books, like something by Richard Scarry, where the entire page is covered with hundreds of little figures all busily working away, except these figures would all be versions of You. Some would be feeding, crying, rocking newborns, others would be lying in bed with the covers over their head, sterilising stuff, putting on laundry, walking round the park, staring enviously at women lunching in cafés with their mates, dressing, bathing, changing babies, wrestling with buggy straps, struggling with car seats, staring in wonder, laughing, crying again, snapping at partners, struggling to fit into a pair of jeans, lying to friends about how well everything is going, tickling tiny chins and standing still in a corner with a speech bubble saying, 'Is it *supposed* to be like this?'

That kind of panoramic view would just about begin to cover the first few weeks Post-Baby, when the landscape of your world, inside and out, has changed so completely that you don't know what firm ground is any more. So much of what you will have been told and expected will turn out to be misplaced, ineffectual or just plain wrong. Unless you're the kind of person who regularly buys into Ponzi schemes or orders Miracle Cure-Alls from the internet, I doubt you will ever before have been intimately involved in such a process of disillusionment as the first year Post-Baby.

The con starts as soon as you conceive, in my experience. All during the nine months of pregnancy, you're encouraged to find yourself *interesting* – to minutely examine every quirk and minor reaction your body has, to muse over your cravings, your revulsions, the state of your skin, hair and nails. And everywhere you go, people are very interested in You and what You need/feel/think. Young men even give you seats on public transport and old ladies smile sweetly at you as you waddle down the street. Society tricks you into believing you have suddenly become fascinating, and you make the mistake of believing this will continue.

When I was pregnant for the first time, I was so damn interesting. It was as if I carried around an Oscar or a Nobel Prize with me for those nine months.

Because I had a bump. And inside the bump was a Baby. Strangers stopped to chat – 'boy or girl?' – and advise – 'oh, it's definitely a boy, with that shape'. One neighbour called by specifically to check that I intended to breast-feed. 'It's the best possible start for your baby,' she said righteously. She and I had lived two doors from each other for years and never spoken before. Old ladies offered remedies for morning sickness – ginger ale, peppermint, dry crackers – and *everyone* got stuck into the 'pain relief or no pain relief' labour debate. Apart from feeling sick and tired, it was a fantastically merry time. Certainly in comparison with what happened next.

Being fascinating lasts until the exact moment you go into labour, when you are suddenly, spectacularly demoted. And once Baby arrives, you're immediately consigned to a kind of also-ran status. You become 'Baby's mother' and zilch in your own right.

Marathon Runners Get a Medal

Let's start with the physical. It's standard issue to equate giving birth with running a marathon, particularly when it comes to post-event exhaustion. Except that after running a marathon, most people are minded, cosseted, congratulated and told to take a good long rest. Some of them even get a medal.

Whereas having a baby, which is at least as physically draining as a marathon race, is simply the overture to the real hard work. You have delivered the baby. Good for you! Now you have to care for it, feed it, change it, stay awake for it, burp it, walk it, worry about it. Gulp! In fact, having a baby is far more like being one of those crazies who run five marathons in five days. Or maybe ninety marathons in ninety days. Except that women who have had babies aren't invited onto talk shows to prattle on about how they trained, what they ate and how they managed such a remarkable feat. Instead, they're largely left alone to get on with things. And trust me, it's the being left alone that's really the hardest thing.

Let's not forget all the attendant unpleasant stuff. You are undoubtedly still sore somewhere, even if it's only your arms from grabbing the gas and air tank so hard you nearly dislocated your shoulder. You will feel mysterious pains deep inside, which you largely ignore. And emotionally, you're like a slug crawling over salt.

Apocalypse Now (and Tomorrow)

First time round, everything is personal. Baby won't feed? It's *obviously* your fault for eating too much garlic and contaminating the breast milk, or holding the bottle wrong, or offering the feed in an unconvincing manner. Won't sleep? You made him over-tired, or failed in the bedtime routine. Won't stop screaming? Oh, that one is easy – Baby hates you, of course.

When your efforts at comforting the yelling child come to nothing, you will feel as if you are being personally spurned. As if a speech bubble had appeared above his or her head, you will just know that Baby is thinking, 'You *moron!* Of course I don't want the soother. Any fool could see I've got an itchy leg and my pyjama sleeve is wet.'

You may also find, as I did, that just by being born and therefore physically detached from you doesn't mean the baby has been uncoupled from your emotional self. Actually, it's a bit like removing your soul from your body, dressing it in a fluffy babygro and bonnet and sending it out into certain danger. That child *is* you, and your inability to protect him or her from what suddenly feels like a world fraught with appalling danger will destroy your peace of mind completely. It will raze it to the ground and you will have to start all over again, slowly rebuilding confidence as you learn to trust that nuclear war will not break out unexpectedly, leaving you to survive in a post-apocalyptic world. That gusts of wind will not appear from nowhere to lift the buggy and baby over the edge of the pier. That wild dogs will not erupt, slavering, from the bushes of the local park and charge towards you.

Because you have never before had so much to lose, your faith is shaken, your bravado silent before the overwhelming realisation that you cannot entirely protect this child. A mother's love should be powerful enough to shake the world, to create Harry Potter's rebound lightning scar every time danger threatens. The sad thing is it can't, and that's where the fear comes from.

You will feel whatever hurt your child suffers, even if it's nothing more serious than a cold wind blowing into their face and making their eyes water, or another, older child laughing at their inability to sit up. The visceral tug to your insides, by the way, will be felt in inverse proportion to the age and understanding of your child.

Everything my first child felt, I felt; when he cried, I cried. Oh, and just to complete the circle, I projected most of what I was feeling onto him. If I thought he would be lonely if he was put into a room by himself or even taken out of my arms for ten minutes, I assumed that he felt the very same, and so reacted with appropriate hysteria to his cries. He could well have been yelling because the light was in his eyes, but I always presumed that instead of a simple, practical matter, it was existential – a howl of pain at the fundamental terror of abandonment.

How useless is that? The poor kid needed someone responsible to be in charge and manage things for him. Instead, he got a terrified, flailing amateur.

'I'm Just Going to the Loo...'

The deep well of love you feel for your new baby will overflow and submerge every other part of your life. You will look at your own mother, and father, in a completely new light. And your partner, instead of being mostly defined in relation to you (let's be honest here), suddenly contrives a magical new identity as the co-creator and protector of this tiny infant. Their aspect, in the light of this relationship to Baby, becomes more heroic and magnificent. But also much more infuriating. Their fumbling inability with tiny sleeves provokes the kind of furious response previously reserved for deep personal betrayals.

The New Parent Myth goes that you and your partner, your Beloved, will find yourselves united as never before, immersed together in the bewitching business of bringing up your child. As with all the other myths of parenthood, it's both true and untrue. There's a connection between you now that's forged so deep it will never work its way to the surface – a ley line that runs from you to him, to the child and back. On the other hand, you may also find yourself shouting at him for spending too long in the loo and shushing him if he speaks above a whisper in case he wakes the baby.

Actually, these days the loo features quite highly in our house as a temporary means of getting away from the noise, mayhem and incessant demands of small kids. 'I'm just going to the loo!' one or other of us will shout, often on a Sunday morning, because it's a legitimate way to escape, one that can't be questioned or thwarted with the suggestion 'why not bring X with you?' in the way a bid to go to the shops might. So off to the loo we go, with a newspaper, not to emerge until the banging on the door has reached a proper crescendo.

Instead of constant harmony around the very best ways to bring up our three children in order that they reach their fullest potential, my husband and I frequently snap and bicker over who did what and whose turn it is to change a nappy. We can be just as nitpicky as a union shop steward confronting a middle manager over job descriptions and benefit allocations, each of us negotiating hard for maximum time off, all while insisting that we have each done more than the other. The fact that we both work from home means we get many opportunities to do this throughout the average day. The backdrop to our daily lives is an awful lot of 'you pick him up, I did it yesterday!'

The Princess and the Frog

In the old days, pre-baby, you could always kid yourself that if your life really started to annoy you, you could just take off, go walkabout, have adventures in the mountains of the Hindu Kush. It was never more than posturing, but the fantasy was quite comforting: 'I don't have to put up with this stuff. I'm going to do hair wraps on the streets of Amsterdam instead…'

Once you have a baby, that little fantasy route is closed. You're tethered.

To me, first time around, it felt like being the princess in the fairytale who has her golden ball returned by a frog, on condition that the frog can go everywhere with her – sit by her plate at dinnertime, sleep on her pillow, be carried in her arms. Yeuch! That story used to make me feel hot and prickly with the horror of never being able to Get Away. No wonder she tries to renege on the deal, except that her father, stout man-of-his-word that he is, won't let her. And then of course Frog turns into Prince and all is happily ever after. All the same, I used to really feel for that princess, stuck with that thing croaking and demanding to be taken everywhere with her. (And I never believed she was able to forget the frog and love the prince. I think she would have always seen a slight bulge to his eyes, a greenish tinge to his skin in certain lights, that would have made her shudder.)

Then I got my very own little croaker, my twenty-four-hour companion. Total claustrophobia kicked in. The sensation of never being able to get away, of being in the iron grip of a tiny tyrant whose needs can only be met by you, and no one else but you, is utterly stifling.

About three weeks after the first was born, someone asked my husband how the baby was. 'Like a good book' was his answer. In other words, unputdownable – literally. I used to long to be able to go away somewhere, just for one night, with no company, no phone, nothing but a book and a big bed. Except what was the point? If I wasn't with him, I was thinking about him, every single second of every single day and night.

In the very early days, the claustrophobia was actually more mental than physical. Even if I did go for a walk alone or out to the shops for an hour, I would be constantly playing scenarios in my head – him screaming, needing to be fed, with a tummy ache or just missing me. Well, that was that bit of R&R ruined. I might as well simply give in and stay with him constantly, because out of sight was never out of mind. Out of sight just meant extra fretting on my part.

In all other human relations, the kind of overwhelming, obsessive love a small child has for his or her mother would be considered unhealthy and dysfunctional, something to be discouraged or reported to the police. And so most of us are entirely unprepared for the intensity of devotion and passion we have suddenly inspired simply by the act of giving birth. It's not that we don't reciprocate – we do, of course we do, in spades – but we also manage to retain one or two outside interests; *EastEnders*, or the weather maybe. Once past the first few intensely vulnerable weeks, we can, with a sneaking feeling of guilt at how pleasant it is, very well bear being parted from our darling babies for a half-hour here and there. Whereas for them (well, mine anyway, usually until they turned two or two and a half), every single time I tried to leave them, even to just go and get a hat from upstairs, was like re-enacting *Sophie's Choice* – icy hands clutching any available bit of my clothing, heartbroken wails of 'Mama! Mama!' following me upstairs.

It's nice to be wanted, but really, I used to long for the day when they would transpose just a little of that devotion onto another object – their father, a rag doll, a toy truck.

You don't fully appreciate the meaning of the word *claustrophobia* until you have found yourself on the loo with a couple of children rattling the door handle, trying to get in; worse still, in the shower, holding the door closed with one hand while a toddler tries to open it and join you, an eight-year-old demands to know what plans you have made for him for the day and a four-year-old yells from the toilet that he needs to be wiped.

It's in the light of those experiences that small things – like driving to the shops on your own with the radio on or having lunch with a friend and no children present – become high points of life.

When my youngest was a year and a half old, I had to go to New York for a couple of days. I was rather lamenting this, moaning that I would miss the children and how tiring it would all be. A friend with kids about the same age as mine chipped in wistfully to say that she would be happy with the plane rides alone. Six hours by herself, able to read and watch in-flight movies, and that at the end she would happily turn around and fly right back again.

Chapter 2

ALONE AT LAST. OH DEAR...

In which I realise that loneliness is as much a part of motherhood as leaking breasts

Child Number One was three and a half, Baby Number Two was less than six months. Both had bugs – nothing serious, just a bit of sniffling, maybe the odd bout of vomiting. No reason to head for A&E, but enough to keep them in the house.

In. The. House. That was the problem. The house was tiny, and after two days of being stuck in it, without let-up, I was starting to think dreamily about running away, with just a small bag of essentials, definitely no phone or tracking device, and possibly never coming back. That was in between staring at the clock. 'Half-eleven? Really? It can't be, it's been hours since I last checked, but then it said quarter to eleven…'

My younger brother, a Trinity student, said he'd come round, mind them for an hour or so and lend me his card to access the brand new college sports complex so I could go for a swim. 'Just walk up to the barrier, swipe the card and you'll get straight through,' he said.

I walked up to the barrier, fumbled a bit, then swiped the card. Nothing happened. I swiped again, even more fumbally. A buzzer went. Not the barrier-opening kind of buzzer, the alarm kind. The lady in the glass kiosk beckoned me over. Heart sinking, I approached and showed her the card, as requested.

She looked at the picture of a handsome twenty-year-old man called Myles and compared it to me, a frazzled thirty-five-year-old woman probably not called Myles. Looked at the picture again, looked at me. Raised an eyebrow.

'It's my brother's card,' I said, face flushing scarlet with mortification. Don't you hate being caught doing something utterly stupid and wrong? 'I borrowed it. I was going to go for a swim, I didn't think it would really matter...' I trailed off.

'I'll have to talk to my supervisor.' Off she went, with the card. Eventually her 'supervisor', an older lady, came back. Stern. 'Now,' she said, one determined to Get To The Bottom of a Strange Event. 'What's this?'

I faltered through my explanation again, mortification growing with every word. Pause.

'We'll have to keep his card,' she said. 'We may confiscate it entirely.'

I burst into tears. Proper, crying tears, not just a few drops rolling down cheeks. There may have been snot as well. 'Please don't take his card, he was so kind to come and mind the children. The baby's sick and we couldn't get out and I thought I'd go mad and it was so sweet of him and he really shouldn't be punished...' I was sobbing now, my whole decades-long pretence of being a competent grown-up entirely given up.

The words *baby, sick, thought I'd go mad* had a magical effect. From starchy to sympathetic, that 'supervisor' had me in a chair with a cup of water, a tissue and some calm good sense faster than I could say 'I'm sorry, I'm being such a fool', which is naturally just what I did say.

'I can't let you into the pool,' she said kindly, 'but we won't confiscate the card, and if you want to join, I'll make sure your application gets processed quickly.' And then, thoughtfully, she added, 'I remember that, feeling like you're alone in the world.'

'Isn't it awful?' We both shuddered.

Being left alone is maybe the hardest thing. The acute isolation that having a very small child brings is physical – your friends may not have babies yet or they don't live close enough, your mother and sisters don't live down the road, your husband is at work all day. But it's also mental. I'm not exactly sure why this is, because it goes beyond the fact that you may not see very many people. It has more to do with the way your entire brain is now bound up with your baby. You have mentally distanced yourself from the rest of the world, the better to focus on this child whose survival depends on you. Presumably nature has very good reasons for this, but the initial result is an abstract kind of loneliness.

In order to step fully into the new world that contains your baby, and function in this world, you need to distance yourself from your old world. With time, the two will mesh perfectly, but for the first months, the effort involved will leave you feeling disengaged from what you used to know and rely on. It's like moving to a new country, with a new language you don't speak very well and some pretty odd customs you need to get your head around.

One friend, a mother of two girls, sighed when I asked what her memories of the very early days were. 'You get up in the morning when the rest of the world seems to still be asleep, and you feel so alone. It's just you and them up and silence, unless they're crying. You feel you *should* be lying on the floor, doing goo-goo and admiring their perfection or doing baby yoga, but you are so tired.

So you're wrecked, but awake, but not really doing anything, but still on high alert. It's just crap. Sorry. It is.' And she's right.

Oh, for the days of communal childrearing, where sisters, cousins and friends would share this tedious task, providing each other with the kind of buffer and reassurance we all need. No one on earth can listen to a new mother, with all her minute examinations of feeding schedules and different types of poo, except another mother at a fairly similar stage of childrearing.

Trust me, not even fathers are *really* that interested, although they have learned how to fake it quite convincingly. No, it's a female commune we need, where children of similar ages and mothers of a like mind can while away days that suddenly seem to have more hours than activities and seem sparsely populated with demands beyond the mundanely domestic. Where once life barely fitted into the available hours, the hours now stretch dismally into the distance.

Like so much else that comes with having children, there's a huge contradiction here. Exactly as one part of your mind is racing with astonishment at how it's possible to be so in love, to derive so much pleasure from simply staring at a tiny hand, to find the whole of life complete within the circle made by your baby's eyes staring into your own as he or she feeds, another part of your mind will be thinking, 'God, I'm bored. I wonder if I could get away even for an hour? Just to the swimming pool? If I leave a bottle and didn't take too long?'

In the absence of the good old days when women did this stuff together, it's an awful lot of tooling forlornly round parks on windy days and making the kind of mental calculations that go, 'OK, if we go to the museum for an hour, and then a café for a bun, that should take us to 4pm and then it's nearly home time, but we did that yesterday and I'm not sure I can face that damn museum again, although at least it's warm...'

And yes, we know it's boring; we even bore ourselves with daily repetitions of 'well, she woke at 11am and fed for half an hour, then went back to sleep until two, woke, fed again, had to be changed, so was back to sleep by three' and so on, ad nauseam. See – you glazed over at that bit. Of course you did.

Even a mother with children at different stages will lose the will to live as she listens to the kind of microscopic analysis of sleep patterns that the mothers of newborns go in for. It's not that new mothers actually find it interesting; rather, these bits and pieces of baby routine are the central fact of our existence for at least six months. Expecting us not to talk about them is like immersing us in a mud bath for months on end, from which we must conduct all our business, but expecting us never to mention it.

Much as we long to have scintillating conversations about the Middle East or Lionel Shriver's latest novel, we simply don't have the time or head space to formulate the thoughts.

What Will I Talk About?

After each baby, my first proper social outing – at night, and with people I don't see regularly, who maybe don't have kids! – was terrifying. And it wasn't the whole thing of fitting into decent clothes again. In my experience, people will forgive you for an elasticated waistband and ballooning empire-line top, but not for a lack of any conversation beyond What the Children Did Today, or worse, the endless road show that is Kids Say the Funniest Things.

'What will I talk about?' I think, in horror. When almost nothing has happened in your life beyond the daily grind of feeding and changing, it's panic-inducing to have to come up with views and observations that were so effortless Before Baby, and will be again. But when your head feels as if it's full of lumpy mashed potato and your life is devoid of any external stimulus or even much clarity, the prospect of talking to someone who doesn't know or care that your baby never sleeps more than two hours at a stretch and that you are therefore mindlessly exhausted, someone who is not intimately involved in the puréeing versus mashing debate when it comes to weaning, is very daunting.

Mothers sometimes complain that their work in the home is undervalued and that no one wants to talk to them at parties. That last bit is probably true, but the reason isn't as crass as you might think. If people don't want to talk to us, it's not because we can't advance their careers or get their nephew a job in the bank. Genuinely, the problem is that mothers are themselves stuck for conversation that isn't child related. Striking up a conversation with Amy, who works in the accounts department of a stationery company, is relatively easy. 'How is business?' you might begin. 'What are the evolving needs of the stationery market?' That type of thing. But a woman who says, 'I work in the home. I have three children' – that can be a bit of a conversation killer. 'How nice. How old are they?' often exhausts the entire topic for those who themselves do not have children.

The sad fact is that even the dizzy heights of delight that mothers experience with their new baby are treated with relative indifference by the rest of the world. The feeling of joy that tingles right through your body, from toes to split ends, when your adorable infant reaches a fat hand out for you – well, the rest of the world is just not getting that. 'OK, you had a baby. Great! Now get over it' is more or less how Society responds. Which is fair enough; we can't all stop spinning every time someone gives birth.

Keep It Commune

The need for a commune of sorts is obvious, and at no time is it more necessary than when you have your first child. With later children, you will have built up some kind of a network – painstaking and possibly inadequate, but it's something – and anyway, the demands of other children mean you can't quite sink into the same two-person pit like you do on the first.

The bad news is that a commune is hardest to come by when you have your first. Even if you're lucky enough to have friends and family who are having babies at the same time as you, the chances are you won't really get it together to see very much of them. You'll be too tyrannised by the next feed or naptime or by the fact that the baby hates the buggy or car seat to actually see any of them. They will be going through exactly the same thing with their own little tyrants, so your get-togethers will happen infrequently and will often end abruptly as a child gets sick on the last clean set of clothes or starts to howl inconsolably, or whatever.

If your friends have slightly older children, you'll soon stop inviting them to come to your house because their suddenly-huge-seeming two-year-old makes so much noise or throws things around and might hit your little angel. If their child is interested in babies, that's even worse. Just as your friend is saying, 'Oh, how sweet. Look, she's trying to give Baby a bottle,' you will be thinking in panic, 'Oh my god, that child just put her fingers in my baby's mouth. I need to get everyone out of here *right now* and disinfect the entire place.' Your heart will race, your breath will come in ragged gasps and you will decide that perhaps boredom is the lesser of two evils after all.

After the first visit or two, it will seem like more trauma than it's worth to have the friend and her wrecking-ball toddler around. So there you are, alone again, with only the ticking off of the New Mother's Mantra – 'napped from 11 till 1, fed at 1.30, probably needs another nap now and maybe another feed by 4pm' – to keep you company. How can so much exhilaration co-exist with such boredom?

By the way, don't expect the new baby to provide any company. Frankly, they are largely oblivious of you except as a source of the things they need. The charming little tricks of laughter, gurgling, pointing and so on that can keep us entranced, if not for hours, then certainly long minutes, don't kick in until about five months. Before that, babies just aren't fun. Mesmerising in the way that a deep, dark pool without much surface activity can be; a natural draw to the eye. But fun? No.

About the only thing that the first baptism of fire teaches you – and this is the most crucial lesson of all – is that nothing lasts forever. Actually, nothing lasts much beyond two weeks, in my experience. Try it. Whatever the unbearable behaviour is – colic-y bouts of an evening, incessant feeding, waking up and yelling at 5am – keep a tally of the days. Chances are, after ten or eleven days have passed, things will have changed. The child may be doing something else that's equally as awful, like sicking up every feed on your shoulder or refusing to be put in the car seat, but at least it will be different. And so, in increments of awkward behaviour, the first months will pass.

By all means, buy a string of amber beads to help with teething or visit a sacro-cranial osteopath to help with the never-sleeping (go ahead, I did; I spent a fortune lugging my firstborn to every crank and quack in town, from homeopaths and osteopaths to naturopaths and seventh sons of seventh sons), but really, these are just ways of passing time until time does its own healing work. They will divert you from the moment, give you the illusion of being in control and being able to effect change and make it all seem to go that bit quicker. And that, with a new baby, is A Jolly Good Thing. Sometimes, it's just about surviving to the end of the day, in the belief that tomorrow will be a better one.

Chapter 3

YOU WILL NEVER BE THE LADY IN THE AD

In which I am confronted by Society's desire to interfere in my life and encounter the concept of Mothershould

Here is a secret you might already have begun to suspect: motherhood is not all it's cracked up to be.

This is not the fault of motherhood, mind. If anything, it's a question of false advertising. Motherhood has been wrestled from the grasp of mothers, tinkered and tampered with, then sold back to us in various new, prettified versions.

We have been disconnected from our own innate abilities to mother well and happily by a whole range of interference. The white noise of media, advertising, advice and social catastrophising ('your children's failures are *your* fault!') has come between us and our instincts so that we no longer feel confident in our role, and therefore we enjoy it far less. Not that motherhood was ever a basket of roses – it wasn't. Your own mother, if she's honest, will have told you this much. But it's trickier now, I'm certain of that.

There is more pressure, more conflicting advice, more idealised images and more general scrutiny than ever before, and we mothers are at the heart of it. We are the thin blue line between the weight of Society's obsession with childhood and parenting and our own children. We are standing in the breach, a target and a buffer, trying to protect them from the fall-out, but ever more eroded in our abilities to do so by the general onslaught.

Because these days, we live in a Shouldocracy – a society based on the principles of Shouldism, addicted to telling us what we *should* look like, feel like, wear, eat, think, in pretty much all circumstances. But when the beady eye of Shouldism gets turned on motherhood, when we start being told how we *should* bring up our children, discipline them and plan for their futures, that's when it really takes off. Because whatever about our ability to resist the endless stream of *should* under normal circumstances, the intense vulnerability of having a baby, of finding ourselves suddenly in charge of something so precious, with so little training and experience in the role, leaves us wide open to the dangling carrot of *should*.

Think about it. How many times have you told someone about a problem or a conundrum you have without them immediately telling you what you should do? I'm as bad as anyone. Let a friend just mention they have an issue of some kind, and before the words are out of their mouths, I'm itching to tell them what they should do.

It doesn't even have to be a problem. Mention that you're thinking of buying some meat, and immediately someone will jump in to tell you that you really should try their butcher because he's so good and not at all expensive…

And Society at large is much worse – more prescriptive, more interfering and more impossibly exacting in its standards. It's like a giant busybody friend standing over us, finger constantly wagging as it butts in with unsolicited advice about what we *should* do.

The Ten Commandments of Shouldism

1. Thou Shouldst embrace guilt and be ready to *Sacrifice All* for your children, even when there is no clear benefit to the sacrifice.
2. Thou Shouldst breast-feed. And always be consistent. And get down to their level when you discipline them.
3. Thou Shouldst use flashcards, bake buns and play educational games.
4. Thou Shouldst Not allow children to watch TV, except educational programmes in small doses.
5. Thou Shouldst cook everything from scratch, and failing that, buy only organic ready-meals that are cutely packaged in bright pouches. Never jars.
6. Thou Shouldst own a sophisticated, streamlined buggy that doubles as a sports car or teleporter.
7. Thou Shouldst look elegant and groomed, even when you have just given birth or wrestled a screaming two-year-old into said sophisticated buggy.
8. Thou Shouldst fill every second of your child/children's day with activities that will enhance his/her chances of success in life. Even though you do not know what life will look like when your child is old enough to live it independently, so picking activities is really only guesswork
9. Thou Shouldst tell everyone that this is the most fulfilling thing you have ever done and you're having a wonderful time, even when you are secretly tearing your hair out.
10. Thou Shouldst keep any reservations you might have about this mothering business to yourself, or everyone will presume you are a failure at it.

When Motherhood becomes Mothershould…

One of the major *shoulds* comes in the form of multiple images of perfection that get held up to us. 'Look, this is what motherhood *should* be. Doesn't resemble your life? Then you're getting it all wrong, my dear.'

These images are a real problem, not just a silly annoyance.

There is an ad that shows a mother breast-feeding serenely in her gleaming conservatory before opting in a mature, reasoned manner to move on to formula milk at an appropriate time – a move seemingly welcomed by her bouncing, happy baby.

The ad is pure fantasy, of course. In reality, those conservatory windows would be smeared with grime and the floor littered with the general debris of getting-through-a-day-with-a-small-baby. The mother would be wondering to herself, 'Is this child ever going to do *anything* but feed? It's only been forty minutes since the last one…' Or she would try to introduce the bottle of formula, only to be met with implacable, screaming, spirit-sapping resistance from the baby.

Take another ad, this time a mother baking cupcakes with her pretty blonde daughter, both smiling into each other's eyes, united in their pleasant domestic task. Reality? Bet you anything the mother would be wincing at the amount of mess being made and struggling not to shout 'I'll do it' as her daughter spills most of the flour onto the counter. Daughter, meanwhile, would most likely be guzzling as much raw cake mixture, with her hands, as she can get away with while Mother moans about her getting worms.

Moving from ads to celebs, as Society so smoothly and frequently does, there's Angelina Jolie showing us all how it *should* be as she smiles with calm wisdom at her brood of children creatively celebrating their individuality and diversity. Reality? She has 20 nannies per child, and if any of the rest of us was *actually* in her situation, we'd be snarling and wondering if we could get away with hiring even more nannies.

These fantasy versions of motherhood are everywhere, and that is the crux of the problem. One or two doing the rounds wouldn't bother us at all. It's the cumulative effect of them, and of there being no other visions of motherhood put forward by Society – except the one in which mothers are failing their children and producing monsters who will go on to destroy the very fabric of society; it's either saints or psychopaths. These images cover every aspect of having and bringing up children from pre-birth until the teen years. (Everything stops dead at about age twelve, when kids are no longer cute and charming. This sounds like heaven to me, but I'm assured by parents of teens that actually, it's weird and disconcerting, like the background noise of your life suddenly being switched off.)

In one way, why should we be surprised? Hasn't every other aspect of our lives – childhood, love, friendship, even walking the dog and cleaning the bathroom – been put through a soft focus lens? An unholy combination of glossy magazines, advertisers and compulsive celebrity watching has conspired to convince us that everything should come with a swirly dress, good hair, a tinkly laugh and maybe a few scented candles. Actual messy, contradictory reality is just too much, so instead it gets whitewashed and fetishised. Why show the subtle, difficult truth when you can get away with a big, shiny, product-selling fantasy?

A lot of the time, it doesn't much matter. By all means, buy into a vision of yourself walking the dog in just the right kind of rustic-but-pretty outfit. Or fall for the fantasy of what your life *should* be as a twenty-something. Look, there you are, surrounded by friends, always out, giddy, merry, drinking too much but hey-you're-only-young-once, Sundays on the sofa watching re-runs of *Sex and the City*. That's all pretty harmless, and there's a good chance that your friends will have fallen for exactly the same kind of fantasy, which means that they will be just as keen as you to live their lives in a manner that looks like it was culled straight from an American sitcom. So you're all in it together, equal partners in Let's Pretend. Jolly good.

Even the media-managed love fantasy, though vile, is bearable. This is the one where He is endlessly spontaneous and rugged, all square jaw and exciting gestures (a bottle of champagne from behind a rock, a surprise trip to Paris), while You are at your most beautiful and mysterious, ever elusive yet delightful. The kind of couple that waiters smile at and other couples envy. It's a bit vomit-inducing and may very well bring its own disappointments down the line, but because you are two consenting adults and whatever you do – whether it's tie each other up with silk scarves and get out the riding crops or smirk at each other in expensive restaurants – is by mutual consent, it's fine.

Where problems really arise is when the fantasy meets a living, breathing, reluctant reality – a baby! Because the lie the images all tell is that a baby can be accommodated into your old life as easily as popping a car seat into a 4x4. In fact, it's more like trying to get another person into a single bed. Your old life has to budge up, move over, make space and compromise hugely. This is not easily done.

So when Mothershould comes up against a baby who doesn't know anything about the image and isn't buying into it, that's when the real trouble starts. Your baby hasn't signed up to the same ideal – you're quite simply not singing from the same hymn sheet, as corporate types might say. And while this not-singing stuff is apparently bad news in corporations, it's a veritable disaster between mother and baby.

In your head, you might see an image of baby having a peaceful morning nap while you curl up beside her and catch up on the day's papers. After that, so the image goes, you might get out for a walk before coming home to a cosy house for a feed, followed by a bit of cooing playtime. If that's your ideal – and I confess that, first time around anyway, it was mine – there's a good chance that you're going to be even more devastated by a day that involves large amounts of screaming, very little sleep, no catching up with anything, whether it be news or laundry, and an hour spent struggling with a buggy round a windswept park while everyone else, or so it seems, is happily doing much more amusing and rewarding things.

Essentially, you have been set up for a giant fall. This is where irreconcilable becomes irredeemable.

Fantasy vs. Reality: The Rematch

Baby is made of much sterner stuff than you or I. Baby is indifferent to the fact that he or she *should* sleep for a few hours every morning so that you can do post-natal exercises and start to look like someone who's 'getting their figure back'. Baby doesn't care that according to your schedule, culled from whatever parenting book you're reading, he or she *should* be sleeping for six hours a night by the age of four months. Baby doesn't care that you've latched onto the idea that combination feeding (breast and bottle) is A Good Thing, again because some book told you it was, and has no intention of accepting a bottle. Utter indifference to all your plans and expectations is the one constant you can rely on.

Babies are incredibly strong willed. I think this comes from single-mindedness of purpose. After all, there is great strength in wanting just one thing. So if baby wants to be picked up, that's all he or she wants. They can yell for it with 100% clarity and determination. You, on the other hand, are hamstrung by possibly having several conflicting ideas and emotions. 'Should I pick him up? Maybe he's hungry and I should prepare a bottle or whip out a boob. Maybe I should just leave him, he might settle. He must be tired, he hasn't slept in hours. I want to pick him up, but if I do that every time he yells maybe he'll be completely spoiled...'

So there you are, expecting to look happy, trim, confident and fulfilled, the way Posh always looks after the birth of her babies; the way the magazines encourage you to believe you can look, with endless articles about fifteen-minute exercise routines *You Can Do With Baby* – but hey, it's impossible because baby won't sleep, has sicked up on every decent thing you own and you still barely fit into any nice clothes because you're so knackered you're eating sugary foods all the time for a bit of energy, so your weight is going in the wrong direction. Plus he terrifies you when he won't stop crying, so rather than glowing with self-confidence, you're wracked by extreme self-doubt.

How do I know all this? Because I fell for it, hook, line and sinker. That was me, with the cute little picture in my mind: myself in practical-yet-elegant clothes, holding a smiley baby, and a few friends, with their own smiley babies, all chatting eagerly about the changes to our lives and how much we relished them. In that picture, I even had myself plopping down a plate of home-baked biscuits (real home-baked ones that I made, not the ones you get in the shop that say 'home-baked' but are really made in a factory somewhere outside Nottingham). The picture was constructed from the multitude of images around me before I actually had a baby.

Now let's put the real picture, the one that actually shows my life, up beside the illusory one.

Oh look, there I am, wearing a stained T-shirt that's too short and exposes my still-bulging middle. God, I look lonely. Well, that's not surprising. I haven't seen another adult in a week, except my sister, who could barely disguise her boredom. I never seem to manage to meet up with my friends because they don't have babies yet and so are at work or are too hung over to move. Or if they do have babies, they don't live anywhere near me. I never get to meet my one friend who does have kids and lives nearby because one or the other of us is always waiting for a nap to start, a feed to end, a nappy change to happen. Ahhh, my baby is asleep in this picture. How sweet he looks. But you can tell from the tense way I'm sitting that he has only just dropped off, and bitter experience has taught me that he'll probably wake, yelling, any minute now…

You see? Two very different pictures, and alas, only the stained T-shirt one is real.

Here are a few other scenarios, drawn randomly from my own life at different stages of having a fairly new baby, where I felt a total failure.

The baby books tell me that I *should* aim to get out every day, because baby and I both need fresh air. But often we don't manage it because I'm too tired, and he hates being in his buggy and howls all the time, so that something that's supposed to be relaxing and healthy just ends up being extra stressful.

I can't figure out when to feed my six-week-old because the books tell me that breast-fed babies *should* go three hours between feeds. But he keeps crying, sometimes as little as an hour after a feed. Is he hungry? Should I feed him? Will he get spoiled and demanding? Should I supplement with a bottle? Could that cause nipple confusion?

I know I'm supposed to purée organic fruit and veg (always starting with veg in the first months of weaning because otherwise my baby will develop a taste for sweet things that will lead – inexorably! inevitably! – to a sugar addiction and obesity in later life) rather than buy the little jars from the shop. But I never seem to have time to buy the veg, and anyway, baby spits it all out and then the stuff goes mouldy in the fridge because who has time to make it fresh every day?

I could go on. For every single scenario in the early lives of my children, there was an idealised version, and then there was the reality. And very often, there was no common ground between those two things at all.

I was probably a bit of a sap to fall for such fantasy stuff, but I wasn't the only one. I asked around about this. These days, I know hundreds of mothers, of all ages, backgrounds and walks of life.

Every one of them has confessed to a similar sinking feeling, often round about the end of Week Eight, when they looked at their lives and wondered just what was wrong with them that they couldn't pull off the effortless success everyone else seemed able for.

I became aware of this only very slowly, a good year after having my first child, and I became aware of it backwards, as it were. It was the growing sense of disappointment and disillusion that alerted me to All Not Being Well. I knew there was a niggling discontent somewhere at the back of my mind, and eventually I tracked it to its source. It turned out to be quite simple – the picture I had in my head of what motherhood *should* look like bore almost no resemblance to the life I was leading. Simple, but devastating. It took me many more years to see that this wasn't actually my fault.

Even now, armed with both knowledge and outrage on this score, I still have to struggle to keep the *should* images at bay and remind myself just how unhelpful they are. My children are no longer tiny – the period of greatest vulnerability to the power of *should* – but I still find myself measuring them and our domestic lives against a fantasy ideal that has been put together by a myriad of different sources, with a myriad of different aims, very few of which are in mine or my child's best interests.

Chapter 4

THE POWER OF NO

In which I propose a jolly alternative to idealised images of motherhood

A birthday party, children of various ages pinning tails on things and guzzling fairy cakes. A heated discussion on sleeping habits and why my eighteen-month-old still couldn't go a night without multiple wakings.

'A really good routine will sort him out,' said Alpha Mum firmly.

'If he's not sleeping, it's because he doesn't want to sleep,' said Earnest-Child-Focused Mum.

'Just give him Dozol,' the woman beside me whispered in my ear, like the subversive gnat in *Alice Through the Looking-Glass*. 'My boys were reared on it.' One of her boys was whacking the birthday child with a balloon sword and the other was rolling under the table in a pair of leather jeans. 'His sex pants,' said his mother, screaming with laughter. She didn't seem very maternal. Not at all the kind of role model I was looking for.

Until she leaned back and said thoughtfully, 'Nothing in your life will ever again be as miserable and grim as this. That's the good news.' It was exactly what I had secretly been thinking, but had never yet dared say. Alpha Mum frowned and Earnest-Child-Focused Mum protested 'oh no, no', but in that moment, this woman was my hero. I just wish there were more of her, more mothers willing to go *off message* and say the worst rather than just think it privately, like eating ice cream in the dead of night straight from the freezer.

So instead of indulging all that Perfect Lifestyle stuff, here's a much better idea. An idea that will make us feel like Superheroes and High Achievers instead of Can't-Cut-It Losers.

Motherhood as Dickensian Melodrama

Imagine if our expectations were the exact opposite – if instead of the smug, glowing picture of perfect mother and baby, Society had presented us with something raw, in grainy black and white, of a dreary domestic treadmill? Something out of Dickens – children wailing, mother with wispy, badly cut hair and a sour expression, a squalid kitchen, maybe even a rat or two.

With that image in your head, every single thing you achieved as a mother, even if it was only to have dinner on a plate rather than straight from the pot while heating a bottle with the other hand, or spending five consecutive minutes chucking your baby under the chin and laughing at him laughing, would feel like a major triumph, an achievement on a par with walking on the moon or discovering Teflon.

Because the problem lies with the contrast rather than with the reality. Take the shiny aspirational image away and put up something utterly dreary instead of it, and our actual lives, which haven't changed a bit, are suddenly going to look fantastic in comparison, like the 'after' bit in a makeover. Looking from one to the other, we will feel dynamic and capable. 'Gosh, I'm actually rather good at this,' we might say as we compare our functioning reality with the rat-ridden fantasy.

Happy, confident and flushed with the success of our efforts, every single bit of those first days of motherhood would be easier and more rewarding.

I would argue that the reality of most people's early experiences of their first baby is more like the Dickensian one than the shiny happy media one. Send us into the breach with the message 'This is hard! Expect to be lonely, bored, frustrated and scared!' and we will be delighted to discover that we are doing so much better than expected. Instead, all we get is 'oh, you'll be tired'.

And yes, we will be tired, but we can deal with that. Because we expect it. We are forewarned, forearmed, ready for it. And because this is the set-piece of new motherhood, this is also the bit people are willing to help with. 'I'll take the baby for an hour so you can get some sleep' is a fairly common offer. 'I'll sit and listen to you as you try and tease out exactly why you feel so overwhelmed and inadequate' isn't. In fact, if you do start to weep and wail, generally some kind soul will say how tired you must be and pack you off to bed for a while. And they're right. But not completely right.

No one likes to mention all the other stuff – the fear, vulnerability, isolation. Not your mother, your sisters, your friends if they had babies before you. I don't know why, because they will generally admit it as soon as you dare broach it, but mostly they won't volunteer the information. I presume this is for two reasons – they may believe they were alone in those sentiments and therefore aren't going to prompt you in case you don't feel the same way. Or possibly they believe that you'll find out soon enough anyway, and why would they spoil your last few weeks or months of innocent anticipation?

I can see their point, but I think we should all speak up.

It could be kept very simple, for those who appreciate dramatics less than I do. A matey kind of message: 'This is a very tough time. You will be challenged and made to feel rubbish in ways you never expected, and most of what you have learned to date will be inapplicable. But you will get through it. After six months you will look back and wonder how you ever survived, but you will be a stronger person knowing that you did. And then you will start to reap the rewards in terms of fun with the infant who has previously been adorable, of course, but also a little bit boring and demanding.'

You could even condense that into an acronym. Something short enough to be tattooed onto our inner elbows so we could check it each time we felt ourselves coming unmoored. Look, here's one:

M   (for Maternal, Meticulous, and Making the best of it)

O   (for On the Other hand, scrap that, I thought this would be more fun)

T   (for This is not what I expected, Tearing hair out and Think again)

H   (for Help, I must be doing this wrong, because…)

E   (for Everyone else seems to be better at it than me)

R   (for a resounding *Really?*)

We could do it in that curly script that sailors and hard men use to write their Mom tattoos, and only we would know what it really meant. Like David Beckham's Chinese symbols.

Just don't bombard us with the message that we are embarking on a magical, wonderful journey chock-full of excitement and delight, because we will be gutted when this is not exactly the case. You might as well give us two mystery plane tickets and tell us to pack a suitcase full of beach clothes and glamorous resort wear, then land us in Lough Derg. The religious Lough Derg, not the jolly sailing one.

You see, expectation is the enemy of happiness. The gap between *should be* and *is* is where disappointment thrives.

Motherhood's Big Day Out

The most obvious way to explain this stuff is the Big Day Out. You have planned a trip – to the seaside, the zoo, a picnic, theme park, whatever. It doesn't matter where or what it is, but you can be certain that the amount of whinging, fighting and tantruming will be in direct inverse proportion to the amount of anticipation that has gone into it. The more you and they have been looking forward to this day, the more sickening your disappointment will be as you survey your darling child or children screaming or sulking because you have refused to buy them (yet another) ice cream or piece of souvenir trash.

If you do not at some point find yourself biting back a variation of 'after all we've done for you, and the effort and expense we've gone to, and all you can do is whinge', well, you are a far better person than me.

This is unfair, really, because the children are just being children – opportunistic, demanding, afflicted with a magpie-like attraction for small shiny things. They are doing what they do. Our disappointment stems from having expected them to be otherwise, to participate in the fantasy of the Perfect Day At The Zoo that we have dreamed up. If they behave in a similar appalling fashion on an average day at the local park, we mostly don't mind; we tune it out because the stakes are low. But the Big Day Out comes with such layers of expectation – a treat, a chance for the family to do something together, a golden memory-in-the-making – so in this case, their deviation from the script we wrote for ourselves becomes devastating.

Once we understand this and learn to counter it with a genuine presumption that all treat days will end in tears and disarray, then there is an excellent chance that we will find ourselves pleasantly surprised.

And it is exactly the same with motherhood. This is the ultimate Big Day Out, with an aircraft hangar-sized quantity of expectation and anticipation attached to it. For the first time in your life, you are truly walking into a parallel world, a magic doorway through which others have passed before you, into a promised land of love. All of that is perfectly true, but if you do not also expect to encounter a whole lot of very dreary, even dark, stuff, then you are in trouble. Come to it with low expectations of instant fulfilment and delight, and you will be very pleased with what you encounter.

Wouldn't It Be Lovely

Because this stuff doesn't work without help from us. Mothershould is something we choose to buy into, consciously or not. The perfect-life fantasies can't take hold without collusion from us. If we ignore them, they don't exist. However, we have let them flourish, and that's why they are now so prevalent and debilitating.

Why? Well, first because we're used to it. We're used to being given images of how our lives *should* look, the kind of car we *should* drive, the kind of storage unit and kitchen we *should* have, so we tend to accept them unquestioningly. Mothershould comes pretty easy after a lifetime of being softened up by all the other stuff.

And because it's nice. We'd like it to be true.

Wouldn't it be lovely if having kids *was* glamorous, endlessly exciting and so emotionally fulfilling that we needed nothing else? But it's not. It's untidy. It involves desperate texts to women we half-know saying 'going to be 10 mins late for pick-up, can you get X for me'. As for emotionally fulfilling, yes, it is. Hugely. But we are still ourselves, and for many of us, there are still more aspects of our lives we want to develop. We do not expel a small piece of our brains along with the contents of our wombs on giving birth (and definitely not the bit that can see the funny side of things), so for many of us, the scope of life, while becoming more focused, doesn't entirely contract.

We wish to be the best mothers we possibly can to this scrap of adorable babyness, but we also want to be successful in our careers and social lives. We want to be ourselves, with the same sense of humour, maybe even a touch of cynicism, that we had before.

So the image is not a truthful one, and the points at which it diverges from the truth are important. Unless we challenge that discrepancy, we are going to find ourselves increasingly unhappy and insecure.

You may think I'm exaggerating, but the more prescriptive Society has become over what mothers *should* be, *should* do, how they *should* look – everything from the correct way to discipline your child to the right kind of nappy bag to carry around – the more impossible it correspondingly is to ever feel confident in the role. And lack of confidence in ourselves is one sure-fire way to be unhappy.

Ultimately, that's what's bad for our children – not the failure to live up to perfection.

Because of all the *shouldness*, we mothers are less honest with each other than we could be about important things. Like how often we shout at our kids or whether we lose our tempers or are impatient. Because shouting, losing our temper and being impatient are 'bad', they don't belong to the perfect world of Mothershould and so we don't admit to them. We wish to present ourselves as creating the optimum set-up in which our children can flourish, so we bury the stuff that could be seen to interfere with this. Which means we're presenting the face of perfection to each other when honesty would be far more appreciated.

We need to cut our losses with the impossible ideal, look each other in the eye and say, 'Yes, I shouted' or 'Yes, I was impatient. I don't feel good about it and hope to behave better next time.'

And then we need to get over it.

We all know that a bit of yelling says far more about the mother's state of mind or inability to handle a particular situation than it does about anything the child actually did. We know this because we've all been there. We might not have actually raised our voices, but hey – we wanted to. A cross word or angry aside is actually shorthand for 'I can't cope with this now. I am temporarily all out of ideas and energy. I need help.'

Admitting it lets us all know that we are normal. Not bad. Not amazing. Just normal.

From there, we can try to do better, gaining confidence from the belief in our own normality in a way we never will if we think we're below-par parents. Believing ourselves to be normal gives us a chance to aspire to be better; believing ourselves to be dysfunctional has quite the opposite effect, a crushing one: 'I'm so crap I may as well not bother trying', basically.

If we can 'fess up to our less than glorious moments and in so doing lower the bar, we are one step closer to a happy situation in which we are open with one another and tell the truth instead of endlessly burnishing a sterile image of perfection.

Imagine that – if we all just told the truth. Didn't whitewash, or varnish, or apply any other kind of paint products to our lives. Didn't try to make each other feel subtly bad by pretending to be more patient, saintly and in control.

Now *there's* a vision.

Chapter 5

WHEN IN DOUBT, GET A GURU

In which I consider the various merits of fail-safe systems, star charts, bar charts and naughty steps

My baby is seven weeks old and I can't stop reading The Book. It has cast a spell over me so strong that even when I force myself to put it down, hide it away from sight, I invariably sneak it out later and read more. I am addicted, craving my next fix of order and routine, horribly fascinated by the vast gap that exists between The Book's babies and my baby.

I am not following The Book's way, you see. Somebody gave me a copy of it, with the words 'this will sort you out', followed by a long story about how she Observed Religiously and her baby slept through the night at six weeks. I stopped listening, on the basis that I didn't have a baby yet, or at least not one that anyone could see without the aid of a scanner, so the tallying of sleep hours was boring and irrelevant.

I flicked through The Book, pre-birth, and decided it wasn't for me. 'Too much routine,' I thought smugly. 'After all, I want a life *outside* Baby too. Why, this book makes it look as if I'll be doing nothing else except tending to the baby all day. Ha!'

Now, seven weeks into the combat zone that is a new baby, it's not that I'm rethinking exactly, but I'm transfixed by the contrast.

The Book's babies, at seven weeks, are being fed at intervals of three and a half hours. The Book's mums are popping off for a rest at noon after expressing a couple of ounces so that someone else can occasionally step into the breach. In The Book, things are calm and pleasant, with needs that are easily anticipated and met. My world and Book world are getting further apart. It's like a mirror held up to the temporary misery of my life – mine is the lumpy, misshapen version of Book world's perfection.

My baby is feeding constantly, randomly, chaotically. He is latching on for fifty minutes, dozing briefly, then screaming barely an hour later. The only thing that will stop him crying is another fifty-minute feed. All told, I'm feeding him every hour and a half, for nearly an hour. And someone said breast-feeding was the 'easy, free, convenient' option?

Meanwhile, in Book-land, the babies are sleeping for six-hour stretches, and more. There is excited talk of them 'going through the night'. Mine is waking every two hours, getting fed, squirming for an hour, sleeping for two, getting fed again…

I am falling into a black pit of chaos and despair. My 'fix' of The Book, like all fixes, is a short-lived high. I get a rush from the notion that this world of order is within my grasp. The Book repeatedly makes the point that a baby can be introduced to The Way at any stage – intoxicating words that keep me coming back for more. 'I could just start today,' I think. 'Just like that. I could have a Routine Baby in two weeks…' Once the rush fades, I'm left dizzy, with a growing sense of failure and discontent.

Because I know I cannot do it The Book's way. It's too different from my way, such as it is – more of a random collection of short-

sighted acts carried out within a defined time span than an actual
Way.

I'm not saying there's anything wrong with The Book. There
isn't. For some people it's a godsend, a lifesaver, the welcome
imposition of order on chaos according to a strict adherence to
routine.

To me, it's a constant slap in the face.

I longed to adopt The Book's methods because I wanted the
results but I knew that the necessary steps were beyond me, mainly
because I couldn't leave the baby to cry for more than a second
without having an adrenalin rush so bad it felt like I was being
chased by African warlords. And because I couldn't get up at 7am.

In The Book, days always start at 7am, whereas at that hour I
was in a deep sleep, making up for the lost hours of the night
before, while the baby, perversely, also settled in for a couple of
peaceful hours. The idea of exchanging that, in the bleak
midwinter, for the intense loneliness of pre-dawn with a tiny baby
made me feel quite hysterical.

The whole thing was wrecking my peace of mind.

Some days, by complete accident or the infinite monkey theorem
(you know, the one about monkeys, typewriters and Shakespeare),
my baby would actually manifest a pattern close to The Book's
babies. He would obviously have shoved a few extra feeds into the
day, but I was ready to overlook that. 'Brilliant,' I would think.
'This is where it all gets good. Soon I'll have time to myself and be
able to plan more than three minutes in advance, because I too will
have a Routine.' And then of course the very next day he would tear
down the fragile foundations of order with gusto and many tears.

Misery!

Until I worked out what looked like the solution –
following The Book – was really the problem. That without the
contrast between this structured, regular life and my gruesome

reality, I would just be muddling through, thinking this was what all babies did, and just getting on with it – a far happier outcome.

So I listened to my mother. I put The Book in the bin (I couldn't pass it on, that would have been like giving someone the One Ring To Rule Them All and not warning them), shut the door on unflattering comparisons and got on with finding a way to be a contented mother to my baby.

Funnily enough, many months later, I picked up a copy of The Book in a friend's house (she had effortlessly followed The Way with her first baby, but the second one was resisting furiously). I flicked through it and discovered that after all that, my baby and I had actually found our own way to The Way, via a lengthy and circuitous route.

I felt like I had just won an Oscar for Best Foreign Language Film, even though my film contained the subliminal message 'burn, Hollywood, burn'.

A Million Readers Can't Be Wrong...Can They?

Surely a book that has sold over a million copies can't be wrong? Or one endorsed by that woman on the TV? Of course it can. It can be wrong for you, wrong for your baby or wrong for your family, as impossible to follow as a raw food diet when you're the type of person who craves steak and chips.

And the 'wrong' childcare book is a disaster. You might as well buy some stocks, sit in them and let strangers throw rotten cabbages at you.

Nevertheless, we all turn to them at some point. How many times have you longed for an 'expert' to simply swoop in and take over? Or just spend a day observing your progress, making notes and nodding silently to themselves, then deliver a report on How You Are Doing, complete with colour-coded sections headed 'Strengths' and 'Must Try Harder'?

Most of us are hard-wired to respond to appraisals and feedback. Without them, we find ourselves floundering around, unsure and lacking direction.

This is when we go looking for help in the form of a guru. Someone to tell us what to do, against whose system we can benchmark ourselves.

The books are almost worse than the magazines and ads, because they give you the illusion of control. The media tells us what perfect mother–baby stuff *should* look like, and the baby books tell us how to achieve that via minutely ordered spreadsheets, or endless indulgence, or whatever their particular *schtick* is. Each one has something to offer, but none have as much as they claim. This is really Making The Most Of Mothershould.

I have a library of them. Books on how to raise boys, how to raise girls, how to raise rats – oh, sorry, that one got in there by mistake – how to raise superstars and happy people. How to parent like an Eskimo or a cavewoman. How to discipline, inspire and feng shui my kids. I have read them all in my quest for help with particular stages of my children's lives. Always the difficult stages, of course. When things are going well, I don't reach for the experts; I trust my own instincts and enjoy the ride. But when things get tough, I immediately presume I'm doing something wrong and go looking for answers. It's the search for perfection that drives me, the need to make everything right instead of accepting that this too will pass.

In general, I have found that the books that try to help me to understand my child's psychology are useful; the ones that tell me what to do aren't. The more prescriptive the books are, the more they promise, the more I mistrust them. Order, calm, predictability, control – this is what they're offering. But is that really all we want our experience of parenthood to be? What about wild, hilarious, ridiculous, inspiring and messy?

Those books that pitch the entire thing as a joyless routine, turning every day into a mind-numbingly specific To Do list broken up into fifteen-minute increments, may offer certainty, but very little fun. By behaving with such suppressed hysteria, they only encourage the idea that there's something to be hysterical about. Surely if having a new baby needs to be tackled like an attic full of rubbish, with a detailed list of how to deal with every aspect of it, there must be something terrifyingly chaotic at the heart of it?

'Be consistent,' the experts say smugly. 'Stay calm. Explain everything to your child.' Well, yes, we can all accept the wisdom of doing these things. Of course it would be much more sensible not to descend to the name-calling level of a three-year-old, but if we were capable of always resisting that particular urge, we wouldn't need the experts in the first place, would we? It's not so much a vicious circle as a vigorous one – an endless round of trying and failing, spurred on by guilt and aspiration.

Anyway, even the experts only ever offer temporary solutions to eternal problems – naughty step, gold star reward system, whatever the latest craze stopgap is. And unless you have a will of iron, they're all ultimately useless. What's that military quote about plans not surviving first contact with the enemy? Well, sometimes children *are* the enemy.

Star Charts and Stopgaps

Over the years, I've tried star charts, marbles in a jar (take one out every time they do something naughty), bar charts with levels that go up and down depending on behaviour, pie charts (literally slices of pie), time out, the thinking chair, the naughty step and many others (these are used intermittently, between my more usual 'system', which consists of yelling 'go to your room' when I finally cross the line between 'exasperated' and 'lost it'). There was a time when I had three sets of charts going at the one time. The kitchen resembled the HQ of a firm of serious number crunchers, working flat out on the most recent census, generating information in a variety of visual forms: flow charts, bar charts, pie charts, candlestick charts, you saw it here first!

I've used these incentives for everything from getting dressed without having to be forcibly removed from behind the sofa to not fighting in the schoolyard. Not one of them works.

Let me qualify that – they all work. For a short time. And for certain very specific things.

Two weeks is the average. In the beginning, the kids themselves are wildly enthusiastic about whatever the New Way is, especially if it's one that comes with rewards for good behaviour. I explain it to them, they ask excited questions, we all feel as if we are powering ahead in exemplary fashion – me towards domestic harmony and good behaviour, them towards the acquisition of more cheap toys. Great.

That is the honeymoon period. It generally lasts a week. Familiarity quickly breeds contempt, and after a couple of weeks their indifference to either the carrot or the stick, along with my weariness around implementation, jeopardises everything.

The day they say 'I don't care' when you warn that they are about to lose a marble or move down a space on the jolly aeroplane chart is the day you know that particular joyride is over.

The incentive system is effective for things like putting pyjamas back on beds after getting dressed or washing hands before dinner. I used a marble jar very efficiently for my middle son when he started junior infants and kept being put on the steps at yard time for fighting. 'Stay off the steps, gain a marble. Five marbles equals a trip to the toy shop.' Simple.

But if the trouble is any more nebulous, the whole thing becomes impossible. Take whinging, the thing that annoys most of us more than most other things. What constitutes a whinge? Is it repetition? Tone of voice? Is it category specific, i.e. it's a whinge when it applies to getting ice cream, but not when it's about going to the park?

Defining exactly what you mean in terms a four-year-old can understand is like picking up grains of sand with your teeth. Whatever system you have chosen will crumble under the impossibility of it.

Even so, I'm not dismissing anything out of hand. Just like the trawl through alternative medicine subcultures – acupuncture, osteopathy, sacro-cranial, healers, amber necklace sellers – the best thing about these various systems of discipline is the illusion they give you of doing something while you wait it out. Something to make you feel you have really started to get a handle on why your little darling has taken to biting children in the crèche, flinging toys at her younger brother's head or clinging to your ankles every time you try to leave the room. Killing time till time does its own work, basically. It's the disciplinary equivalent of a cup of tea before the bus goes.

Chapter 6

Two's Company

In which I discover that two is easier than one, but only just...

'After the first death there is no other,' wrote Dylan Thomas. I think this holds true for birth. Nothing will ever top the sheer strangeness of the first time you are handed your own baby, covered in blood, vernix and glory. However, that doesn't mean it's all plain sailing from there on.

The Baby with Two Brains

My second child, another boy, was born at 8.30am on a Sunday morning and we came home from hospital that evening at about 6pm. As I was feeding him, I noticed a squishy swelling to one side of his head, which is not at all the sort of thing you want to notice on your newborn baby.

That looks a bit odd, I thought. My husband thought it looked a bit odd too, so I rang the hospital, got the midwife who had just discharged us, and said, 'It's me again. What's the squishy swelling on the baby's head?'

'Ah yes,' she said, 'that's a cephalohaematoma. Nothing to worry about, very common; it will go of its own accord in about six weeks.'

I didn't ask for any more information. Once she said 'nothing to worry about' and 'go of its own accord', I got on with eating a dinner fit for twelve men and went to bed.

The next day, the squishy lump was bigger. I wondered why no one had thought to mention it to us before we left the hospital. The day after, it was bigger again. I wondered if there was any chance the midwife was wrong about it being a cephalo*whatsit* and 'nothing to worry about'. It continued to grow, reaching critical mass – about the size of half an orange – on day five, and I continued to wonder.

I did eventually do some research – apparently it was caused by a build-up of fluid between the skull and periosteum membrane, and was probably the result of a fast delivery.

Every day for a week a different midwife came to check up on me. 'Ah yes,' they all said, looking with curiosity at the squishy lump, 'a cephalohaematoma. Nothing to worry about, very common; it will go of its own accord in about six weeks.'

Meanwhile, I had taken to keeping the poor little thing literally under wraps, with a hat on when anyone visited, because I didn't think he was doing himself any favours with that weird lump. I thought no one would realise how cute he was, they'd all just say, 'What's that on his head?' Sure enough, any time I took the hat off, someone would instantly say in shocked tones, 'What's that on his head?'

My husband called him 'the baby with two brains' and slyly pointed out after a week or so, 'All the doctors and midwives say it's very common, but have you noticed that none of them say they have actually *seen* one themselves before?'

My mother wasn't at all reassured by the 'nothing to worry

about, very common, it will go of its own accord' mantra. 'I think you should take him to see a doctor,' she said, daily.

'But I *have*. He's seen two paediatricians, two GPs and nine midwives. They all say the same thing. Nothing to worry about, very common, it will go of its own accord.'

'Well, I think you should see another doctor.'

Eventually, at about six weeks, exactly as predicted, it started to go down, picked up speed and disappeared entirely in about a week. Now the dear little baby had just the one brain, like everybody else, and finally visitors began saying, 'Ah, isn't he sweet?'

And all the while, Baby himself was angelic. He was so sweet, and sleepy. Such a good little fellow. My initial feelings for him were intense protectiveness, followed by deep gratitude at his goodness, and finally, after a couple of weeks, I was astonished to find how much I loved him. This exponential increase in love amazed me, because I had presumed I would have to stretch what was already there a little further, like pastry over a pie dish that's bigger than you thought. Instead, it was like the bliss of an elasticated waistband after a day poured into a pair of leather jeans.

But all the same, I was astonished to find how tricky it still was. You would think that we would get better at coping with the series of GUBU emotional and physical happenings that accompany a new baby. Well, the good news is that we do. The bad news is, not by much.

When I had Baby Number Two, I expected more from myself. More perspective, more sanity, better stamina. Second time lucky, I thought. Second time happy – an opportunity to enjoy having a tiny baby in a more relaxed way, without the frantic, fear-filled ignorance of the first time.

This time, I was sure I would have everything I needed and wouldn't be buying babygros on a weekly basis as various growth spurts took me by surprise, or not be thinking vaguely that I should get one of the blinking, winking toys that croon lullabies, only to find that the baby was suddenly ready for jigsaw puzzles. I would understand the rhythms of a tiny baby better, and so would be able to nap during the afternoons instead of lying awake waiting for a cry; wouldn't be caught with a hungry child in the middle of town because I'd rashly believed I had time to nip in and buy a bath thermometer. This time, I was certain, everything would go according to plan.

A friend of mine calls this the Second Baby Delusion – the feeling that you actually know what you're doing, that you learned so much the first time around that you will be able to navigate the stormy post-partum waters with ease. It is this delusion that sees you heading merrily off to the shopping centre on Day Three, with two small children and the airy notion that it will all be fine. 'I am Mighty Mom, I can go to Dundrum!'

You can't. Try it and you will end up having a very public meltdown, begging someone to air lift you out of there.

Second Baby Delusion is followed by Third Baby Realisation – that you have learned nothing of any value except to stay very close to home, keep your head down and ignore the buoyant lies told by your hormones.

I also presumed that I had learned so much about guilt by then that I was inoculated against it. That the first child had been the dose of cowpox that would proof me against smallpox. Now I know better – I know that guilt, just like love and the elasticated waistband, is capable of exponentially increasing.

A New Baby Is a New Baby

In making these happy calculations, I was forgetting one crucial thing. A new baby is a new baby. As in, it's not a baby you've ever had before. It's a new baby, with a new personality, a new list of likes and dislikes, of fears and wants, a new body clock and new reactions. And you have to learn all these things the hard way. Is this a baby who wants to sleep all day and be fed all night? A baby who hates bath time? Is startled by sudden noises? Does she love or loathe the car seat? Music? Bright lights? You will find yourself obsessing over the patterns of a tiny infant all over again, usually managing to establish what those patterns are immediately before the infant changes them and sends you back to square one.

And the second time, you have something else to contend with – the slow-burning fuse of discontent that is the first child's reaction to a new baby. The thorn in the side of delight.

'When's That Baby Going Home?'

My first child was devastated by the appearance of the second. He was kind and sweet to the baby, but very keen to find out when it would be leaving, and to make sure it wouldn't take any of his things with it.

'I know, Mummy,' he said one day, having hit on the perfect solution. 'We can give the baby to Aunt Bridget. She can mind it.'

Once he realised the baby wasn't going anywhere, he started to shout – at everyone. His voice went up several decibels overnight. It was shock, I think; like Marie Antoinette's hair turning white. He kicked against anything I asked him to do, usually literally. He transferred all his affection to my husband, sending him from basically a zero to total hero, in one swoop. After all, his father hadn't let him down as catastrophically as I had. Hadn't broken his heart by adopting a small leech that he seemed to insist on wearing constantly about his person, like a fetching new scarf.

The Loneliness of the Long-distance Mother

Yet again, with a tiny baby, I felt acute loneliness. Only this time I was lonely in a crowd, physically surrounded by other people – often too many other people – but psychically lonely. Because the new baby owned me – as thoroughly as if I had put my soul up in a card game, and lost – and could claim me at any stage. One wail, and I was lifted out of whatever activity or engagement I had been involved in, even if that was playing with my eldest or listening to him explain just why he needed to put his toys down the toilet.

Mostly, I felt lonely for this eldest son, even when he was right beside me, because we were no longer uniquely bonded. The connection between us had frayed and stretched. I was a long-distance mother; he was metaphorically out of arm's reach. The child who had until a short time ago seemed so small and delicate was now a hulking monster in comparison to the new one. I missed our carefree times together, without the new baby to come between us. I missed his complete devotion and the trust – now broken – that he had reposed in me.

I hated having to keep telling him 'in a minute, when I've finished feeding the baby'.

After a couple months of this, I told my sister Bridget through tears one night that if I had known just how badly the eldest was going to take it, I would never have had a second child. And at the time, I meant it.

What a wuss, right?

These days, I have a rather more robust attitude, based on the Utilitarian calculation of maximum good. In offsetting the trauma of displacement against the benefits of having a sibling, I'm inclined to find in favour of having a sibling. It wins, but only just.

I tried hard to keep this in mind when Number Three came along, a girl this time. By then the second was nearly four, and I reasoned that, never having been an only child, his reaction to a new sibling would be far more muted than that of his elder brother to him. Instead, again almost overnight, all his solemn certainty was displaced by a shrill bid for attention. He became violent in all his actions, including the affectionate ones. He no longer felt like the centre of the world, so he fought for what he used to accept as his right. His new way was to grab for love with gritted teeth and shower it on the baby with identically robust emphasis.

He started to make up words to describe emotions that were totally new to him. 'Can I goji the baby?' he asked, constantly. 'Goji-ing' meant putting his hands around her tiny skull in an apparent display of affection, then straining against the urge to squeeze so hard that his whole body trembled with the effort, all while he smiled maniacally and shouted how much he loved the baby.

The thing about kids is, they're not very subtle. When they act out, they leave a thick trail of clues behind them. There are many similarities between sociopaths and very small children. Actually, the only real difference is 20 years and about five feet.

Disconcerting as the playing out of displacement activity can be, I actually much prefer the hurly-burly of family life to the precious, intimate interaction of one-on-one.

Breaking the Magic Circle

Yes, there is something incredibly sweet and touching about the bated-breath adoration of two new parents. The constant solicitous little touches, checks, conversations. 'Do you think she's warm enough?' 'Should I move him out of the sun?' 'Do you think I should wake him to feed him?' 'Just move that blanket a bit, will you, it's touching her face…'

Adorable, but stifling.

I know Nature makes it so, but the deep selfishness of new mothers is pretty hard to take. I was as selfish as anyone. I thought the entire world revolved around me and my little baby, and if it had come to a fight over precious resources – a crust of bread, a dry cave – I really dread to think how I might have behaved. When it came to cherry-picking the choicest morsels from a communal meal – a roast of lamb, say, or pot of stew – for my own little darling, I was utterly determined, like a Jewish mother from a joke, and indifferent to the sidelong looks of friends or family.

I do see that there is a place for this in ensuring the survival of the species, and thank goodness it seems to die down a little after the first, but that contracting of the world right down to baby-size, the narrowing of focus to exclude anything that isn't your offspring's welfare and the assumption that everyone else is on the same damn page – well, it's a solipsism too far.

Even at the time it felt unnatural, unsustainable, too intense. For all the displacement grief, I actually much preferred the later babies, when family life couldn't be stopped and rerouted for the convenience of the littlest, because by then there simply were too many others. The baby had to adapt and join the onwards-rushing stream, with no chance to sit in a little cocoon for a few months. By then, the family unit seemed like part of a wider world in which we were all invested. Hell, I would have fought for crusts and comfort for any of the kids I knew by then.

And yes, two is company. Three even more so. Even though, with few exceptions, being talked to by small children is a bit like being trapped by the party bore, the guy who can't read the signals that you couldn't care less about the county council's obligations regarding cycle paths. Except for the fact that the child is more likely to be droning on about the superpowers of Dr Doom versus the Fantastic Four and which is stronger, a lion or a cheetah, it's a very similar experience. You can't get a word in edgeways. The fact that your attention is unengaged matters not one whit as long as you are physically present – standing in the same room and saying 'mmmm' once in a while is enough. Your active participation in the conversation is unimportant, as is any notion that you should enjoy it.

It is crushingly boring, but hey, at least it's conversation. Something a tiny baby, for all their adorableness, cannot supply.

The Law of Diminishing Arts and Crafts

The thing about the precious one-on-one time, though, is that it isn't all gazing and gooing. There's a lot of painting, reading and chatting that goes on too. All the things the baby books recommend, in fact. But those things are subject to a law of diminishing returns, and by the time you get to Baby Number Three, for example, there's very little of this dedicated activity going on. Look back at Baby Number One, and you will find him or her, in your mind's eye, surrounded by Things You Never Did Again.

The CDs of baby songs, the flashcards, animal snap and memory cards are all there. Most of all, though, it's a sea of art materials. We all force ourselves to break out the glitter glue and egg boxes with the first so that they can explore their creativity and experience the magic of finger painting, but after that, not so much. I know any number of mothers who simply chucked the contents of the arts and crafts cupboard in the bin once the second child was able to say, 'Want paint, Mama.'

'I outsource it,' one mother told me frankly. 'I can't bear that stuff.' In fact, there's a woman who lives locally to me who makes what I fondly imagine to be a *fortune* by doing this very thing, and only this thing. She gets a gang of kids round, at €8 an hour each, and lets them *paint*. And glue. And put glitter and sequins on stuff. I think she even let them stick bits of macaroni and lentils to paper.

She certainly fills a niche. All those mums tortured with guilt over their child's creative development but hopelessly squeamish about mess are able to reap the best of both worlds.

So very little of that one-to-one stuff happens after the first that it's kind of a miracle that subsequent children learn anything at all. But they do, and often quicker than their siblings – because they're busily learning from those siblings, of course.

Knowing this, I am currently operating on the same kind of principle as the very old days among poor folk, whereby only the eldest child could be spared to school. He then came home and taught the younger ones what he had learned. Translated into my family life, I'm hoping that all the years of dedicated input into the first will pay off as he transmits these things, via the mysterious telepathy of children, to his siblings.

Get the first right, I figure, and the rest will follow. Like pancakes.

Chapter 7

BREAST IS ... BREAST

In which I breast-feed for three years before discovering that it isn't a cure for cancer or the fiscal crisis

My eldest was about two and a half. Old enough to have a few words. Old enough to put some kind of vocal coherence to what he wanted. Old enough to know his own mind very clearly. Way too old to still be breast-feeding.

So when he began pulling at my top on the DART, saying 'want a feed', I tried to distract him. Out of the corner of my eye I could see a Quite Famous Musician I half-knew begin the shimmy that would precede a routine of 'Hi, how are you, what have you been up to? Is this your kid? How sweet. I'm just on the DART because my car is broken' or 'I was too wasted last night to drive home'. That kind of thing. Then he noted the increased struggles going on in my berth and sat back down again, turning his face firmly to the window so we could both pretend no one had seen anything.

'Want a feed!' Now the child was tugging at my top, trying to pull it first up, then down as successive routes of entry were barred to him.

'Oh look, there's a birdie. And a dog. *Wow*, a dog!' My desperate attempts to distract him were not working. Why didn't I bring a biscuit? I though desperately. Even a king-size Mars bar, a bottle of wine. Anything to prevent him from sticking doggedly to his current purpose.

'Want a feed!' It was getting menacing now. The contents of my bag offered nothing in the way of alternative entertainment. The whole carriage was watching us surreptitiously. Society doesn't approve of two-year-olds breast-feeding. Tiny babies, yes; children old enough to express their wishes with actual words, no. The Quite Famous Musician, bless him, had turned right around in his seat and was staring fixedly at a point on the outside horizon.

'Want a feed! Want a feed! Mama, want a feed!' Cheeks scarlet with mortification, I gave in. What else was I to do? He wasn't going to. Top up, bag arranged with as much discretion as its small size provided, child latched on, making – God help us! – lip-smacking noises of satisfaction as I stared out the window, palms sweating with embarrassment.

That happened pretty regularly. Usually without Quite Famous audiences, but still. My extreme-breast-feeding wasn't a 'choice', really, in that it wasn't the product of sitting down with pen and paper one afternoon and weighing up the pros and cons of the situation:

Pros
So very good for them
Cheap
The WHO says until two years old at least and who am I to go against the WHO?

Cons
Embarrassing
Impractical (I don't have the clothes for it)
Age inappropriate (him, not me)
Makes me look like I grow my own wheat grass and am planning
to home school him when actually all I want is a quiet life
Embarrassing

The Baby–Boob Contract

It just wasn't worth the battle to stop. My first child was deaf to all
efforts to slowly inch him in a more socially friendly, bottle-based
direction. And I wasn't up for several weeks of hysterical crying
while I weaned him off.

We already knew, he and I, who was the boss of me, so I didn't
engage in a battle I knew I couldn't win. I managed to cut him
down to one feed before bedtime and one in the morning. I worked
around it. Literally.

When he was two, I had to go to Cannes for a couple of
days, to the immense TV fair there. For work. It should have been
jolly and glamorous, the kind of jaunt I would have killed for pre-
baby. First I ruined it (and annoyed everyone) by whinging about
how much I was going to miss the baby. Then I forgot a breast
pump.

Of course I forgot a breast pump. The child was two. I hadn't
looked at one in at least a year. When not actually with me, he was
perfectly happy to be given a bottle or drink milk out of a cup. It
was only when I was around that he demanded the stuff on tap, so
I hadn't bothered with the miserable business of expressing for a
long time.

The trouble was, no one warned my boobs that they weren't
required to perform up to their usual standard. That they could
slack off and go on half-time. They continued producing their usual

quantities, as stipulated in the Baby–Boob Contract. Except no one was collecting the stuff.

After a day, I looked like one of those South American women who get cheap boob jobs, probably from their dentist, or greengrocer, or maybe a man who goes round door-to-door and does the whole family, mother and daughters, as a job lot. Huge, rock hard, starting under my chin and jutting straight out in an aggressive shelf of solid flesh. And oh so painful. The agony.

I could not begin to concentrate on what I was meant to be doing – selling the idea for a new TV channel to a load of documentary makers from across Europe. All I could think about was had I started leaking (yes), could everyone see this (yes) and what the hell was I going to do for the next twenty-four hours? Expressing by hand was of very limited usefulness and I simply didn't have time to go scouring Cannes for chemist shops that sold breast pumps. Who knows if French women even pump? Bet they don't. Plus how could I explain to my all-male team of colleagues why I needed to disappear for a couple of hours? After all, I was the mother of a two-year-old, not a tiny baby.

There's a bit in Colette's *Claudine à l'école* where a girl is excused from school because she has to go relieve her sister's aching boobs now that the baby has been weaned. Utterly disgusting, but I might well have agreed to a bit of similar assistance in those moments.

Somehow I got through, got home without actually exploding (without successfully selling the TV channel idea either, but I'm not sure that was my fault as much as the fault of the TV channel being un-sellable) and resolved to put weaning higher up my to do list. Definitely before tidying the shed.

It's Not a Magic Potion

And now there's a new wave of research to suggest that breastfeeding may not even be all that good for them after all!

Now obviously I need to qualify that, and fast, before I get threatening letters from those who believe it's the elixir of life.

Breast-feeding is very, very good for babies and mothers. It is by far the best option for feeding small children and it protects to some degree against breast cancer. No one doubts or disputes this, least of all me. In the developing world it can literally mean the difference between life and death.

However, there is no actual trustworthy scientific proof for many of the benefits claimed for it. Yes, it reduces gastrointestinal infections. It may also mean a lower likelihood of childhood allergies, asthma, obesity and ear infections, but this has not been conclusively proven. It may mean you get back into your pre-pregnancy jeans a little quicker (of course, it may also *not*; it's far too easy to while away those hours on the sofa with a cup of tea and plate of chocolate digestives) and avoid the post-partum blues. But again, these things have not been satisfactorily proven by randomised controlled trials, the way they should be before we all start shouting about them.

This much I can tell you: breast-feeding cannot make your child a genius or give them super-health. It cannot put men on the moon or solve the financial crisis. It does not prove that you are a better parent. It is only breast milk, not a magic potion or a magic bullet.

Oh, and it's also not free, despite what the public health nurse told you. It's not free because you have to do it, and while you are doing it, you will not be able to do anything else, except maybe read *Heat*. This means you may be paying someone else to clean your house, even mind your older children, while you feed. And the trauma of your existing child or children at having to share you with a new sibling will be compounded by the fact that you can barely put the new baby down. Being constantly told 'in a minute, I'm just feeding the baby' would make any normal child feel justly furious. You might even be spending money on feeding-friendly clothes. And that's all perfectly dandy, but let's not ignore these facts in our rush to convince everyone what a brilliant idea breast-feeding is.

Claiming too much – 'Breast-fed Babies Have Higher IQ' screams one headline; 'Breast-feeding Better for Bonding' screams another – in order to persuade more women to do it isn't helpful. That kind of hysteria never is. And encouraging guilt about it for mothers who don't do it is definitely bad.

I can see why the breast-feeding folks do this – it's a great pity that more women don't breast-feed, and for longer – but I can't imagine that hyping up the claims and loading on the guilt is really going to help. I mean, I don't like it when people oversell to me, even less when there's an implied threat: 'Send this email to five people today and you will have amazing luck. If you don't, bad luck will come to you.'

Quite off-putting, no?

The Tip of the Iceberg

Even the bad news gets turned into good news. A study that made headlines in 2012 was that breast-fed babies showed more 'challenging' temperaments (and we all know what 'challenging' means when applied to babies). They apparently cry more, laugh less and are more irritable. But the study carefully ascribed this 'challenging' carry-on to the 'dynamic communication' between mother and baby, going on to say that bottle-feeding is like 'comfort eating' and produces babies who may be quieter because they are over-nourished. Sedated, you see. Stuffed so full of easily accessed milk that they don't respond.

So heads we win, tails you lose.

Now I'm not the greatest fan of 'studies'. They're often badly conducted, misleading and flatly contradicted by different 'studies'. They are the tea leaves of science.

In fact, many of the currently unproven claims for breast milk
are the result of being unable to untangle it from the other trapp-
ings of concerned middle-class mothers. Because it's voluntary, the
result of a decision, we are automatically talking about a certain
type of mother – mostly middle class, very child focused, determined to 'do what's best' even when it entails personal sacrifices.
Exactly the type of mother who also plays educational games with
her children, is careful about what she feeds them, reads to them
and so on. Who's to say any one of these things, or what's more
likely, a combination of things, isn't responsible for whatever health
or IQ benefits her children manifest?

And now I think I'd better say it again in case you missed
my first avowal and are getting ready to send me hate mail – I
am all *for* breast-feeding. It is of proven benefit to mothers
and babies. It is perfectly designed by nature for its purpose
and cannot be improved upon. It may not be free, but it's mighty
convenient and doesn't require you to ask waitresses to heat it or
sterilise it. It doesn't run out (unless you're very tired and your
baby is going through a major growth spurt, and even then,
running out is temporary). It is all the good things and everyone
should try it.

And that is quite enough to be going along with. We may yet
find proof that breast-feeding makes babies more enlightened and
'indigo', or that it's like the Ready Brek glow and protects from all
manner of ailments. I wouldn't be a bit surprised. But until we do,
let's stick with what we know and work from there.

Because of all the emotive discussions around childrearing, this
one has to be tops. Whether or not you breast-feed says *everything*
(apparently) about the kind of mother you wish to be. It's a kind of
bodily semaphore that mothers can wave at Society: 'Look, I'm
breast-feeding. I'm a *good* mother. I will make sacrifices for my
child. I will tend to their psychological development and play

games with them. You won't find my kids running feral through housing estates when they're older.'

We are demonstrating it to the world at large, other mothers and even to ourselves. The more we sacrifice, the more we believe that we are doing the best for our child.

It's a kind of emotional currency in the bank; damage limitation. We can offset the sacrifices made in breast-feeding against our failures in other matters. 'OK, I shouted a couple of times and wouldn't pay for that trip to Kathmandu, but hey, I *breast-fed* you. I gave you the best possible start...'

One reason why breast-feeding is so militant in the States is because it tempers the guilt of working mothers who have to be back at their desks after six weeks. That's a pitifully short maternity leave, and yet women mostly have no choice but to accept it, so they sublimate their guilt over leaving the child into an insistence on pumping. That is a sacrifice they can make, something that's within their power. And so they sit there, doing something that's very boring and dreary, buoyed up by the belief that they are still helping their baby. That even from the distance of the lactation room in work (if they're lucky enough to have one), they are still ensuring the best possible outcome for that child.

I know this because I was that soldier. I felt that if I could just ensure that not a drop of formula touched my child's lips, then I would be making it up to him for having to leave him. The cost to myself was considerable – exhaustion, not to mention the law of diminishing returns, because breast-feeding is a supply and demand thing – but it was better than the psychological pain of feeling like I had abandoned him.

The thing about breast-feeding is that really, the actual boob – the bit you can see – is only the tip of the iceberg, if that's not too odd a metaphor. Beneath the tip is an entire enormous weight of supposition, identity, lifestyle beliefs and aspiration. And so it's not enough that it's A Good Thing to do, here and now – it also has to be mythologised and invested with sacred powers that carry into the future. 'Your baby will be healthier now – and cleverer and better adjusted later.'

By that same token, if you decide not to breast-feed, you are denying you child far more than breast milk. You are apparently denying them the chance to excel in later life.

It seems unfair to beat someone with a stick that is largely made up, but still hurts. And that is what is happening here. Attitudes to breast-feeding are a microcosm of our culture of risk avoidance, an invisible barometer of Best.

Chapter 8

EVERYONE BLAMES THE PARENTS

In which I learn more than anyone needs to know about guilt

If anyone asked me to name the defining emotion of mother-hood, I would probably start to gush about joy and love – and I would mean every word of it. But even in full flow, a slight niggling would start up at the back of my mind, because what comes with all the joy and love is a close cousin of these two emotions and is maybe impossible to disentangle from them: guilt. Guilt is like a parasite that lives on joy, burrowing into and contaminating it, and could well be the most consistent, if not the dominant, emotion of motherhood.

The guilt is relentless and inescapable, and it starts, in my case anyway, almost instantly. I do the little test and my first thought is, 'Oh my god, I'm pregnant. How wonderful!' My second thought is, 'Oh my god, how much did I have to drink last weekend?' That first wave of guilt is only the beginning. Through the course of the pregnancy and then into the early years of childhood and beyond, the guilt changes, waxes and wanes, but never departs entirely.

All those cupcakes I haven't baked, all that finger painting I haven't done. The unmade homemade play dough, the unplayed educational word games. I don't even know whose vision of motherhood it is that I'm failing to live up to, because most of my friends and the other mothers I meet claim to be the same – all just trying to get through our busy days without significantly short-changing anyone except ourselves. These mothers don't bake or finger paint either, yet this fantasy vision of life reproaches us all. It's Martha Stewart's vision, maybe, or Nigella Lawson's. Not mine. So why on earth does it have such a hold over me?

The seductive image of me wearing a cute flowery apron, baking biscuits at a sleek kitchen island with my two boys, the Aga gleaming in the background and the stereo playing brain-expanding Mozart symphonies while we all rap our way through jolly little number games, is a powerful one. Even though we don't have an Aga, or an island.

When I do bake with the children, they fight over who gets to lick what while I hover anxiously, fussing that they'll get flour everywhere or spill the sugar or that the biscuits will be lumpy. Which makes me feel guilty for not being able to relax and go with the flow.

Which means that not only am I feeling guilty about the real things that I've done wrong or not done, but I'm also feeling guilty about the unattainable and imaginary. I'm feeling guilty about an imaginary vision that I haven't managed to reproduce. I know it sounds ridiculous, but I'm perfectly serious.

Express Yourself

I went back to work when my older son was five or six months old. I was in a state of devastation about leaving him, madly resentful towards the whole of society for making it necessary, and the Lotto in particular for not turning up my numbers and sparing me this pain. I was also determined, with the gritted-teeth conviction of the chronically under-slept and slightly crazed, that return to work would not mean stopping breast-feeding.

Every day, I busily expressed breast milk in the loos at work. At the time I was editing *The Dubliner* magazine and our offices were above the International Bar on Wicklow Street. This meant that yes, the loos were above the International Bar too, and we shared them with the comedy club on the middle floor.

Ah, those loos.

Every morning in the office would start with drawing straws to see whose turn it was to go and check what condition they were in. Some days, that condition was so bad that Intervention was required. This took the form of popping downstairs to the bar and whispering to whoever was on duty there that the loos 'needed a bit of attention'.

At which point, the barman would sigh heavily – who could blame him? – and fetch a mop and bucket. There were days I privately thought he needed a power hose and decontamination suit.

Really, those loos were revolting – rarely clean, often filthy – so what the hell was I doing disappearing into them every day with a breast pump and a little plastic storage bag to express enough milk for my son's next-day feed?

Why didn't I just give him a bottle? God knows. I was so sold on the idea of Breast Is Best that it never seriously occurred to me. But also – and I see this clearly now, in a way that I couldn't see anything at all then, even if it was five inches in front of my face – I was over-compensating.

I felt so miserable and guilty about leaving the baby and going back to work, so certain that my departure was damaging him in some fundamental way, that this ridiculous expressing became a kind of token of my continued devotion. And the harder and more unpleasant the whole thing was, the more I felt I was doing him good. Like the way artists feel they must suffer to produce great art.

He might have been out of sight, but not out of mind. In fact, far from it. Some creepy book I'd read on expressing recommended picturing your child's face in order to encourage the let-down reflex, so there I was, in the foul loos, intently visualising my dear little baby. Yeuch!

Even now, I cannot understand why some kindly person didn't take me aside and say, 'Let it go, love. Just give the child a bottle of formula and give yourself a break.' Sadly, no one did, although I did get some funny looks from friends when I told them what I was at. Much later, one friend told me that hearing of my efforts – absurd and heroic in (almost) equal measure – made her feel terrible for stopping breast-feeding at four months when she went back to work.

You see? None of us can win.

Most of us mothers are prey to this kind of hilarious, awful guilt. It's something that goes with the territory. You can't turn it off – well, I can't – but recognising it for what it is is a start, a step towards developing a much-needed sense of humour, something that will be of more use than any parenting manual in the world in getting you through.

Recognition is also the first step in realising just how much Society is colluding in our guilt. After all, whose rosy-tinted images of idealised motherhood are we being peddled? The Renaissance painters have a lot to answer for here, but in more recent times, I bet you anything it's a twenty-something childless guy in an advertising agency.

Pick a Battle, Any Battle

Right now, this minute, I feel guilty, in no particular order, about the following:

- My children eat too much pasta and not enough green veg.
- I haven't organised swimming lessons for them.
- I owe too many playdates.
- I don't take them to museums and galleries often enough.
- I let them watch too much TV and don't monitor what they watch closely enough.

I also feel guilty that I don't spend 'quality time' with my husband, haven't repainted the boys' bedroom in the subtle shade of sage green that I chose off a chart about two years ago, let the older one wear Astroturf runners every day instead of 'proper' shoes because I can't face the fights, and countless other petty things. These things niggle at me; they crowd out the corners of my mind and interfere with my enjoyment of family life. They are the shady places in an otherwise quite sunny world.

There are other times, when the balance of family life is more disrupted – if one of the children is going through a particularly ornery phase, as happens periodically, or working life steps up a notch or two. Then the level of guilt tips over into something much more intense. At these times, I start to think about Long-Term Psychological Damage, Emotional Insecurity and the Life-Long Effects Of An Inadequate Childhood. In capitals, just like that.

I'm sure I exaggerate all this, but the feeling of gloom that comes over me when I snap at one of the kids because I'm tired, plonk them in front of the TV because I'm busy or ignore them because they're whiny and I'm irritable is enough to keep me awake at night.

I know that this kind of guilt is irrational and self-indulgent. As a freelance writer married to another freelance writer, I know damn well that when I have to worry about how I'm going to afford their school books and health insurance, I don't bother too much about the more nebulous issue of their psychology. But being able to not worry simply because one shouldn't has always been beyond most of us, and so I still lie awake sometimes, replaying the scenes in which I have failed to be patient and tolerant over and over in my head, squirming with shame.

The A to Z of Guilt

Actually, I could just have called this chapter The A to Z of Guilt:

A is for Alcohol, the drinking of, and Annoyance, the giving in to.

B is for Breast-feeding, of course, and the good start you will be denying your child if you don't.

C is Childcare and the Choices we are all supposed to make around this; for Cupcakes unbaked and Creativity unencouraged.

D is for Dog, child's best friend, and the refusal to get one. For Discipline and our failure to instil it. For Dinnertime and how we're all supposed to have it together, every night.

E is for Education, are they receiving the best?

F is for Fish Fingers, the heavy reliance on, in place of 'proper' meals. Fresh air and lack thereof in their lives.

G is for Getting out more, the need to do so. For Good enough and wondering if we really are. For Guilt, of course.

H is for House, which bears no resemblance to interiors magazines; 'Hurry up', which we say too often; Help, the lack of; and Habits, bad, that we are letting them get into.

I is for I and the way it isn't in 'team' and is only at the end of 'family'. For the Inability to Implement, mostly in the field of 'proper' boundaries.

J is for Juggling, natch. For Job if we have one, and 'Jeez, look at this mess' if we don't.

K is for Keeping one's temper, the failure to.

L is for Loneliness, Laundry and the piling up thereof.

M is for Maternal instinct and the limits thereof. For Manners and the failure to instil.

N is for the Naughty Step, and how on earth does one use it?

O is for Other mothers and how much better they are at this.

P is for Peace of mind, Proper food and Playdates, none of which are functioning as they should. For Photos we haven't taken of the second child.

Q is for Quality time, the lack thereof, with both children and partner.

R is for Regrets, we have a few, and Reasonable tones of voice, which we so often lack. For Routine, which we struggle with.

S is for Swimming lessons, failure to book. Soothers and not getting rid of them earlier. Self-esteem and whether we are encouraging the optimum amount. For Sleep, of course, now and always.

T is for Time and how quickly it passes, so that we should be appreciating everything more, now.

U is for Understanding – them, us, our relationship, their tantrums, the way they scribbled on that wall for attention.

V is for Vitamin D and the patchy supplementation thereof. For Versus (nature, nurture) and for Variety, the lack thereof in our daily lives.

W is for Where did it all go wrong? What was I thinking? What now?

X is for Xbox and all the other things their friends have that you refuse to get.

Y is for You-time and how there isn't any. For Young, which they only are once, so it should be magical.

Z is for Zzzzzz, the exhaustion of feeling constantly guilty.

Chapter 9

AND THE PARENTS BLAME THEMSELVES

In which I accept the inevitability of guilt but try to offload some of it anyway

An afternoon at my mother's house, when my eldest child was about three. All went well until I refused to allow him to pop the lenses out of her glasses. He looked at me solemnly. 'You've been nothing but a pain this afternoon,' he said.

'I wonder where he learned that?' my mother asked tartly.

There was a time before my elder son was born, now glorious in retrospect, when nature was winning the age-old battle with nurture; when the way your kids turned out had less to do with you than with their genetic predispositions; when the responsibility for their adult happiness and sanity was shared more equally between parents and their parcel of inherited traits. There was great freedom and relief in that. As a parent, you weren't the only blame-game in town; you could even attribute all the bad bits to nature.

Now that comfort zone has shrunk away to almost nothing.

The most up-to-date thinking is that the ball is firmly back in our court, and so our failures or otherwise as parents will resound down through the years.

I can see that this is mostly A Good Thing – that our children are not predetermined to exhibit the same traits as their parents, that they get to start with an almost pristine slate, but when I think how quickly we parents start to muddy that slate, I panic.

Just when the obsession with parenting – motherhood in particular, of course – is at its highest, when the degree of navel-gazing over childrearing and the various 'choices' we apparently make is most intense, we get dealt the knockout blow of greatly increased responsibility as well.

Everyone *is* watching, everyone *is* judging and it *is* all our fault.

Fallen Madonna

Until recently, no one expected anything much of mothers beyond that they physically care for their children. Feed them, clothe them, cuff them round the ears to teach them a lesson, and there you were! I mean, not so long ago we used to put children up chimneys and down mines because Society believed that they could be co-opted by their parents for whatever end suited those parents. We (grown-ups) owned them (children), as it were, and were free to use them any way we wanted: for saving crops, shoeing horses, cleaning houses, bringing in dowries. Now, it's far more likely that they own us. Our respect for them – for their feelings, for the autonomy of their persons, for their wishes – has grown exponentially, and rightly so. The idea that one would lay violent hands on another simply because that Other is small and can't stop us is totally dated, and the rejection of that idea is a kind of shorthand for a whole lot more. In general, we are more considerate and thoughtful of children than ever before. We do not rule their lives with the same kind of autocratic insensitivity that was normal for generations. We don't even do that thing of spitting on a handkerchief and vigorously scrubbing their faces clean any more (anyone who remembers the indignity of *that* will know that we are headed in a much better direction).

However, the flip side of our excellent greater sensitivity is the way in which we are taking the whole business to heart. Now that the responsibility for their happy outcome seems to lie so squarely with us, we're like butterflies on a piece of card, squirming on the pinpoint of guilt. This is particularly true of mothers.

Generation Game

On top of everything else, I suspect that we are the first generation to feel that we are doing this *worse* than our own mothers. For a long time, no one much cared about bringing up kids. It wasn't an art and a science, the way it is now. Then, when it did start to become important, each new generation had the authoritarian, repressive, undemonstrative example of their own parents to react against. Anything they did was better than what had been done to them. But that all came to a halt with my generation, because we are the daughters of women who were very good at mothering. They had read Dr Spock. They knew – unlike the generations before them – that babies need love and attention, not cold prams down at the bottom of the garden.

We're not crummier people than our own mothers, not at all, but we do have a whole lot more on our plates. And those plates are no bigger than they used to be, just more crowded. Jobs, careers, Brazilians, being sex goddesses and style queens, having a working knowledge of the situation in North Korea and the novels of Hilary Mantel, and so on. We look back at the fairly leisurely way in which we were brought up, by educated, enlightened, financially stable stay-at-home women, and contrast it with the frantic dash between crèche, school, work, extracurricular activities, supermarket and salon that we're engaged in. Our own upbringings seem coherent and ordered in a way that our mothering does not. That could just be a trick of perspective, but alas, I suspect it isn't.

That feeling of being worse is joining the tide of Shouldism directed towards us and fuelling the secret sense of guilt and inadequacy that runs through so many of our lives. Too often, we quietly accept this as our lot. We shouldn't, because it's not accurate. Yes, we are different from our mothers and we have to manage our lives in ways that they didn't, but if we only focus on all the negative little ways in which we are different (less time, correspondingly less patience), then we are going to miss the great excitement and potential that is also part of our new deal. Our world is not perfect. There are too many 'choices' to be made, particularly around out-of-home work, that turn out not to be much of a choice at all, but our horizons are far broader than those of our mothers.

Guilt by the Pound

Child psychology as a discipline really took off only in the 1960s, and since then the role of the mother has become increasingly ridiculous. It was always fetishised to an extent, particularly culturally – all those lovely paintings of mothers looking down serenely on sleeping infants, a small, mysterious smile playing about their lips – but the kind of microscopic scrutiny of what, when, why and where, leading to an impossible checklist of things we're supposed to do and not do, is new.

A straw poll of other mothers I know shows that they feel almost constantly guilty. Not all about the same things – the ones who care less about nutrition than me couldn't give a hoot what their children eat, as long as it's plentiful and reasonably unprocessed, but they might be tortured over the lack of sun holidays or their failure to disinfect the house from top to bottom. Others agonise about the lack of a sibling for their child, even when this isn't something they had any control over. For others again, it's the limited amount of time they get to spend with their kids that dismays them, even though this too is usually beyond their control.

The type of guilt is obviously specific to personality and circumstances. In my experience, the stay-at-home mums are more likely to tie themselves in knots about the strategic quality of after-school activities (Suzuki method violin, anyone?), whereas those working full time are bogged down in negative reflections over missing bedtime. But details aside, the actual quantity of guilt seems fairly standard issue: 'Here's your helping of guilt, Ms Mother. Dispose of it as you choose.'

The question is: is guilt ever helpful? Is it always destructive? Is guilt nature's way of ensuring that we take extra care, or just a poisonous by-product of the social bombardment around what mothers *should* do and be?

The Illusion of 'Choice'

Let's look at one of the thorniest and most guilt-inducing of all issues for a moment – childcare. I love the way discussions about childcare focus on the 'choices' we mothers have apparently made, when the reality is that most of us simply do whatever seems to make sense and is possible. We don't sit down with a list of possibilities – crèche? nanny? part-time work? au pair? – and sedately work out what's best for our child. Instead, we look at our (usually) limited options and pick the lesser of several evils.

Money is usually the key determinant here. If you work full time and aren't lucky enough to have a cosy arrangement whereby Granny will do a couple of afternoons a week or some other ad hoc permutation, you're basically stuck with choosing between a nanny and a crèche. And there's a price difference of about double. That would make most people's minds up pretty fast.

There are plenty of reasons to pick a crèche – they're plentiful, reasonably well monitored and reliable. A crèche is never going to call in sick because it has a cold 'and doesn't want to pass it on to the child', which is the kind of excuse I've got from many a child-minder over the years. (As far as I'm concerned, pass it on! Just don't spring a sick day on me at short notice.) Nor is a crèche ever going to supersede a child's parents in his or her affections, which is a major concern for some people. When I recall how much my middle son loved his Brazilian nanny, I can thoroughly sympathise. Three years after she left the country, he is still talking about her. 'Deane used to do that with me,' he will say wistfully, obliquely aware that the pinnacle of his care was reached somewhere between eighteen months and two and a half years.

There are also plenty of reasons not to pick a crèche, including fears about the quality of care and increased media muttering around the idea that children under three who spend long hours in day care apparently grow up to be more aggressive, disruptive and disobedient. The fact that the media muttering is so agenda driven (basically, the opposition attacks the government's childcare policies, rolling out whatever 'expert' supports a robust counter-argument, because they know very well that these things grab headlines) makes it very difficult to sort sheep from lambs on this one.

Maybe long days in a crèche aren't a great idea for small children. They certainly stink for parents. I imagine most would avoid them if it were possible, if only to spare themselves the horrors of early morning drop-offs with cross, sleepy children and the charming process whereby crèches will fine them a fiver a minute for late pick-ups. But making these parents feel miserable and guilty isn't going to help. Encouraging them to explore and afford other options is. Failing that – and so far, Society is totally failing – shoring up their confidence as parents is a far better idea than undermining it.

Where choice is an illusion, surely guilt should be optional?

My own childcare arrangements were as capable of reinvention as Lady Gaga. I don't think my elder son had the same set-up two days in a row. Some days he had both parents around, other days, when we were both busy, he could easily find himself minded by three different people in a day. All these people loved him and minded him beautifully, but how confusing to be handed from pillar to post, and no wonder he took to dragging a bear called Pooh round with him everywhere. That bear was the only real consistency he had.

By the time the second, and then the third, were born, we were a more child-focused family and had a bit more money, so they had a regular minder who came every morning. Even so, it took many tries to find someone who was any good. First there was a nice American who came maybe four times, then simply didn't turn up and changed her mobile number. After her came an Irish girl who was fantastic when she was there, but called in sick so often – usually on a Thursday and Friday, for some reason – that I began to fear for her long-term health prospects. The next one tried to renegotiate her hours and pay after the first week – hours down, pay up. And then we tried a time-share with another family, only to find that the permutations of illness where five children were involved were simply impossible. The sheer text burden alone was giving us arthritis.

Each change was violently precipitated – because the old way was ending – and determined by the various combinations of hours needed/ money available/ minders willing. Choice? Nah. Crisis management, more like.

Beyond Instinct

Wouldn't our job as parents be so much easier without guilt? If we trusted ourselves and just followed our instincts? I think we would generally know what to do. But we're way beyond our instincts on nearly everything; we don't eat when we're hungry or sleep when we're tired. So instead of mothering out of a natural understanding of our children and their needs, we read books and articles, watch television programmes and draw up charts, trying to crack the mysterious code that is childhood as if we needed a map.

The result is that we second guess ourselves and lack confidence. We're inconsistent because our approach depends on whatever guru we're following at the time. All we want to do is our best, but how on earth do we do that when we have no idea what it should be? Do you spare the rod and risk spoiling the child? Or just spoil them and to hell with the rod?

Expectation has an awful lot to do with it. Our expectation is that we will bring up our children with endless patience to be wise, intelligent and loving people; that we will enjoy the process and learn about ourselves as we teach them; and that along the way we'll have time for all the extracurricular niceties, like those cupcakes and homemade play dough. It's all a far cry from the slightly frantic, awkward, guilt-ridden process that most of us are involved in.

We mothers don't have time to meander through the days, our children learning at our knee how to whittle or milk a cow, while we too learn, at the same forgiving pace, how to be the best mother to that particular child. There is always another deadline to be met, a collection or drop-off to be done, shopping to be got, meals to be cooked, another child's whining to attend to. Modern life to be lived, really, whereas tiny children are probably better suited to the rhythms of the cave and the campfire.

We're Not That Stupid…Are We?

This is the guilt about not being perfect enough, not living a life in Farrow & Ball. Being less than the vision of motherhood that is dreamed up in a thousand marketing departments all over the world and sold back to us mothers. Guilt over an unrealistic ideal? Please! We're not that stupid.

Except that we are, or can be. We all feel it sometimes, but the more aware we are of where it comes from, what it's based on – a fantasy notion conceived by some overpaid male marketing exec in a corner office somewhere – and how little it has to do with the realities of our lives, the easier it will be to banish it.

Like the Bogeyman, the best remedy against this spectre of unmerited guilt is laughter. Laugh off that vision of the beautiful smiling mother in her dream kitchen with delightful compliant children while a fat ginger cat suns herself on the windowsill between the pots of homegrown herbs. Turn instead to your own noisy, chaotic, possibly muddy house, with your own adorable, ornery children, who might be watching TV, playing Wii or flinging bricks around, and embrace it. They are your reality, and you are theirs. Could anything be more beautiful?

Our Children Are Not Our Children

The idea takes some getting used to, but essentially, I think the prophet Kahlil Gibran was right:

> Your children are not your children.
> They are the sons and daughters of Life's longing for itself.
> They come through you but not from you,
> And though they are with you, yet they belong not to you.

Realising the truth of this is a hard thing. When you have fed, changed and protected a child, stood between it and discomfort, distress and disappointment, it is very difficult to realise that you don't actually own him. For all the love and care you pour into that child, he doesn't belong to you. He belongs to himself.

We all have the entirely admirable, if impossible, desire to see our children uncorrupted into adulthood – the desire to encourage the best in them without infecting them with the worst of ourselves. We dearly wish to give them our love but not our thoughts, to pass on to them what we have learned without also passing on the stains of our own failures. Tragically, this isn't possible and we have to learn to accept that.

They will pick up our insecurities, foibles, phobias and false consciousness just as surely as they will pick up stomach bugs and colds. We cannot be near them without influencing them, and that influence will not always be for the good. And this in turn makes us feel guilty when we see them behaving with all the (temporary) petulance, aggression and irrationality they have learned at our knees.

We need to get over this, accept it and move on because this transference is just a fact of life and therefore not worth dwelling over. It's as much use to get upset because it rains when we want it to be sunny. Of course we can, and must, try to minimise the extent of our cross-contamination – work through our own wretched hang-ups as much as possible in order to understand and temper them – but in the meantime, we also need to trust that our children are getting a diluted form of these hang-ups, mediated by all the good things we give them as well.

So yes, I'm transmitting a certain impatience to my children. I can see it happening. I can see it in a horribly familiar tightening of their mouths when they say, 'Come *on*, I've been waiting for hours' or 'I've *told* you not to do that', but they're also getting (I hope) healthy doses of self-mockery and self-awareness, and a dawning hint that their impatience is ridiculous, just as mine is.

I'm teaching the good stuff by example, just as I'm teaching the bad stuff. If they can learn one, they can learn the other.

Chapter 10

Yummy Mummies

In which I explain why Demi Moore has a lot to answer for

What exactly is a Yummy Mummy? Simply put, it's a woman who is slim, glamorous, well-dressed and with good hair. And a child, of course. Even more simply put, it's a woman who looks as if she has borrowed someone else's child for an hour or so and will shortly be giving him or her back.

There are also such things as MILFs, but let's not get into that.

Back to Yummy Mummies. Not an average mother then? Alas, increasingly yes. This gleaming paragon is to be found more and more at a gym, coffee shop or school gate near you, and she is upping the ante for all of us in a most irritating way.

Because on another level, Yummy Mummies are a particularly nasty, invidious media construct aimed at undermining the rest of us mothers and giving us one more thing to feel guilty about. You may not have expected the language of an angry sociology major in this book, but sometimes such language is called for, and this is one of those times.

Not so long ago, we were perfectly happy as Mammies. The heart of the nation. Strong in the face of endless adversity. Built, and dressed, to last. The Irish Mammy was an icon for all the years this country was a poor and blighted place. A self-sacrificing tyrant, her son's inspiration and obsession, perfectly indifferent to daughters. The sentimental songs and stories eulogising her are only equalled by the jokes mocking her – 'How many Irish mothers does it take to change a light bulb? Oh don't mind me, I'll just sit here in the dark.' These days, you'd be hard put to find a single Mammy out there under the age of sixty. We just don't make 'em any more.

Motherhood by Stealth

Before we go on, let me say that of course it's nice to look nice. We all feel better about ourselves if we reckon that we look good. But, I would argue, with a large bump or small child, this should be our choice – something that might happen once a week, even once a month, when we make a special effort because we're meeting friends or going out with our long-suffering partners. The rest of the time, we should glory in the freedom to wear an old sack if it pleases us.

And yet, ever since the media came up with the notion that being pregnant or having small kids is really no excuse for looking grotty (if not, then what the hell is? Terminal illness?) and coined the cute little phrase 'yummy mummy' to heap shame on those who persist in carrying on as if it were, wearing old sacks has become quite controversial. At exactly the same time that Society is telling us there can be no fulfilment for women without children ('Look at her, CEO of a major company, driving a brand new Lexus and holidaying in the Bahamas. No kids. Poor thing, she must be so lonely…'), it's also shrinking in horror from any physical evidence of having those children at all.

Motherhood by stealth: leave no traces. You need to look like the one in *Desperate Housewives* who pretended to be having a baby (she wore a fat suit for a few months) in order to cover up the fact that her daughter was. So she went away, took off the fat suit, reappeared with a cute little baby and no other signs of birth. Perfect.

Pregnancy used to be a time when you could legitimately hide, pile on the pounds and expect a little kindly indulgence from those around you. For nine months up and nine months down, smocks were acceptable, à la Princess Diana pregnant with William, or even American-style 'sweats' and comfortable shoes. You were beneath the notice of the fashion police, and because you were generally dressed down, there wasn't much point going for the perfect blow-dry and manicure either, so you were relatively free to just duck your head and get on with being pregnant; a kind of necessary but unglamorous cog – a D- in the Brave New World of Procreation.

Underneath that shapeless smock, it was generally assumed (by anyone who wasted their time thinking about such things) that your body was similarly shapeless. For whole centuries of human existence, that was perfectly fine. Entirely normal. For thousands of years, a diaphanous layer discreetly shrouded women and their childbearing. Participation in one of the two Eternal Mysteries (life, death) meant that Society was willing to cut us some slack in the arena of physical appearance.

There have always been a few men who fancy pregnant women, but they are mercifully thin on the ground. For most of the world, being visibly pregnant was always like having a benign force field around you, a kind of bubble that repelled unnecessary attention. Either people offered to help – seats on public transport, carrying shopping, a fan when your brick-red face looked ready to explode – or they politely ignored you. And for most of us, that was lovely.

But in the last fifteen years or so, the rules have changed. And many of us are still struggling to catch up, and wondering why on earth we should.

The Naked Truth

If you ask me, it all started with Demi Moore posing naked, seven months pregnant, on the cover of *Vanity Fair*. She wasn't just naked, she was also ridiculously toned and shiny and slim, except for an absurd round bump, like a python that had swallowed a bowling ball, or one of those hors d'oeuvres composed of pickled anchovies and olives. Of course they airbrushed it, but I have a horrible feeling that the original images weren't a million miles from the published version.

That lifted the veil a little. Thanks, Demi. Don't these celebrities ever stop and think that their acts of self-promotion are moving the goalposts for the rest of us and that we can't go back? Or at least not unless the Taliban invade and start to impose a little order.

For the celebs, the steps are probably small and logical (in their crazy world anyway). 'I've just broken up with my husband/boyfriend. I need to show the world I'm OK with it, so I'll dye my hair blonde and bag a hot toy boy,' they might think. Or 'I'm about to turn thirty in an industry that thinks this is grounds for euthanasia, so I need to show that I'm still incredibly fit and virile. I know – I'll pose naked and preggers.' All well and good for them (and indeed, the strategy worked very well for Demi – in the years after that *Vanity Fair* cover she made *Indecent Proposal* and then *Disclosure*). For the rest of us, though, something subtle shifted forever. An expectation around what we *could* look like was created, because when the game is changed in this way, we're always moved forwards, into the terrain of *more* exposure, *more* revelation, *more* expectation. A taboo is broken, a new marker is put in the sand, and within a few years what was really 'out there' becomes normal. And the rest of us are expected to adapt and catch up.

And so, post-Demi, pregnancy gradually became more than just a private matter. It's not that magazine editors were clamouring to put us on covers or take snaps of us naked. Rather, the expectation around what one should look like while pregnant shifted. You can't just be a blob any more – you have to be fit, svelte, groomed, count calories, exercise, eat raw foods. Basically, you have to look 'normal' *and* 'pregnant', like the models wearing 'bump suits' who get booked to appear in ads targeting pregnant women (it's like actors 'blacking up' in the old days, and should be just as frowned upon). These two things should really be as mutually incompatible as 'asleep' and 'awake'.

Salons even offer Brazilian waxes to women reaching the end of their pregnancies on the basis that it will be one less thing to worry about once the baby is born. Personally, worrying about the state of my bikini line was not at all high up the list of priorities – somewhere below 'must find matching bedside lamps for spare room', in fact.

Seeing ads for pre-delivery Brazilians just makes me think (apart from 'ouch!') how hard we fought for the right to give birth with a full bush. It used to be routine to shave women's pubic region pre-delivery, not because anyone thought it looked nice, more *groomed*, but in order to offer a better view to the gynaecologist, and to hell with the fact that it grew back all itchy afterwards. Women eventually won that battle on the grounds that it wasn't strictly necessary and could lead to minor infections if the skin was nicked. After my first baby was born, my mother was more delighted with that bit of news than nearly anything else. 'So ugly, just like a skinned rabbit' was her description of the unexpected sight of her own pubic region.

And now we have reverted, by choice, but for different reasons.

Mainly it's a generational thing. Women under thirty find pubic hair just as impossible as the rest of us find underarm hair. They think it's unhygienic and gross. I think it's a nice little covering of an area that's not particularly aesthetically pleasing and needs a bit of camouflage. And unlike underarm hair, no one gets to see it except those who are expressly invited. And presumably they – well, *he* – is too dizzy with delight at the invitation to be judging. Plus I hope he has nothing to compare it to.

In fact, I refuse to jump up and down with delight at the 'choice' this apparently represents in the lives of women. It seems to me, all disingenuous talk of 'empowerment' aside, to be just another way in which our lives are being clogged up with extraneous *stuff* that shouldn't register at all during such a time.

Couldn't we have a total grooming amnesty – a gramnesty – for nine months?

Dressing the Bump

Melanie Blatt (the pretty one from All Saints who wasn't a sister) did another bit of marker-moving in 1998 by leaping around on stage, pregnant, wearing a kind of crop top with exposed, rounded belly while she sang, 'Never ever have I ever felt so low. When you gonna take me out of this black hole?' I quite admired her attitude – 'so what if I'm pregnant, I'll wear what I want' – but my mother, who does not shock easily, was truly appalled by the sight. She could not understand how anyone would be so blatant about something that, to her and all previous generations, was so innately private. In fact, she was so alarmed by the kind of role model Melanie might be that she hot-footed it over to visit me during my first pregnancy with a suitcase full of discretion – long, flowing, soft things – lest I be tempted to do an All Saints.

These days, of course, it's impossible to go onto any news website without endless pictures of naked celebrity bumps – Beyoncé, Kim Kardashian, Shakira – but back then, Melanie's bare-all attire was pretty brazen and kicked the whole question of what to wear when you're expecting up a gear.

In some ways this was a very good thing, because loads of shops got in on the act and began stocking cheap and cheerful ranges for pregnant women. And even though it's not all about shopping, this was heaven.

I think I can date when this happened – it was sometime between 2003 and 2006, i.e. between my first and second child. When I was pregnant on the first, there was nowhere to shop except dedicated maternity stores, which were expensive and incredibly depressing (think baggy leggings with elasticated waistbands and *Little House on the Prairie*-type flowered dresses; you were doomed to look like an earth mother or a middle-aged tourist). I couldn't afford to kit myself out with a whole new wardrobe and was seriously uninspired by what was on offer, so I looked like a rag-bag for months on end.

In fact, come to think of it, I had a very badly dressed first pregnancy. I looked awful. My husband's glamorous cousin gave me a couple of Diane Von Fürstenberg ruched dresses that she had worn during her own pregnancies, but I decided that they were much too good to actually wear, and stretch. So I hoarded them until post-baby, as something to look forward to – the sartorial equivalent of the parlour or 'good room'. By the time I was pregnant with Number Two, there had been a merciful mushrooming of maternity lines in all my favourite shops, and the whole notion of 'dressing the bump' suddenly became quite fun.

That was the good side of the growing media obsession with pregnant women. From invisible, we were suddenly all the rage. And I do accept that it's a good thing not to feel that we need to hide, creeping around in the shadows, just because we're pregnant.

But there's a serious downside too, because we now have to look the part – glossy, glowing, groomed. This is all part of a general trend of excessive grooming that is deeply tedious, but even more so, I would argue, when you can't see your feet, let alone put polish on your toes or spend longer than twenty-five seconds getting dressed in the morning because small children are clamouring for you, than it is for the rest of womankind.

The expectation of looking good carries a heavy weight. What starts with Yummy Mummies can end up in body dysmorphia.

Jean Genie

There's a whole thing around jeans (no, not genes, which it really should be at such a time) during pregnancy which many of you will be familiar with. It's the notion of how quickly anyone can get back into their pre-pregnancy jeans, like that's the ultimate test of worth. It's hilarious and pathetic in (almost) equal measure. And I was no more immune to it than anyone else.

During my first pregnancy, part of the reason I looked so rag-baggy was because I had serious issues with the notion of putting on weight and a tragic determination to stay in my normal jeans until the bitter end. I didn't, of course, but I did squeeze into them for about eight long, constricted months. I think at one point I could hardly move, the waistband was biting so tightly into my flesh. But it was all worth it because I could answer friends who asked 'are those your normal jeans?' with a smug 'yes'.

I would like to go back in time, sidle up to that idiot in her too-tight jeans and hiss 'Boo!' into her ear so that she jumps and finally pops the button. But it wasn't just me, you know. I recall seeing a rather gorgeous radio producer I vaguely knew being interviewed about her pregnancy a few months after I had my first baby. There she was, happily boasting that her only concession to pregnancy thus far – about seven months in – was one pair of size 10 low-rise jeans (I could almost hear women throughout the land gnashing their teeth). I laughed. But grimly, you understand, like a woman who has Seen Too Much.

Part of the pressure of not putting on weight is so that you have less to lose afterwards and can slip back into your pre-pregnancy jeans even quicker, thereby earning a round of applause from your friends, who are just as idiotic as you about this stuff. Now that I think about it, I definitely cheated a bit. By wearing the damn jeans for so long during the pregnancy, I stretched them hugely. The getting-back-in was consequentially much easier. Ha! Not that I admitted any such thing at the time, either to myself or anyone else. Nearly all my girlfriends commented (not always approvingly; some of them are much stronger-minded about this stuff than I am) on the return to p-p jeans, because women do not miss this stuff.

By the second pregnancy, I had mostly got over the sad fear of looking fat. I confess that I always rushed to tell people 'I'm pregnant, you know' the moment it was decently advisable, lest they – God forbid! – suspect me of putting on weight, but at least I no longer lied by saying I was a few weeks further along so that I would seem smaller than expected. And if you are choking into a cup of tea after reading that, I don't blame you.

In fact, for the second and third pregnancies, just to over-compensate, I went a bit weird the other way and began wearing enormous clothes when I was still barely showing. As I recall, I was in full-on maternity gear from about three weeks. I think it must have been my own private penance.

You may have worked out from all this that I have a bit of a problem around the idea of my weight. Well, I do and I don't. I do, in that I do think about it, quite a lot, but no more than anyone else. Fat is a female issue, and very few of us are immune to the fear of it. But chuck that general low-lying-weight-obsession in with the disappearing comfort zone of invisibility that used to exist around pregnancy, and we can see a real problem developing well beyond the normal anxiety over weight gain that so many of us have.

Pregorexia, or 'mommyrexia', as they dub it Stateside, is a

growing disorder: women exercising madly all through the pregnancy (there are now scores of websites devoted to selling work-out gear for pregnant women, while sizes for maternity clothes these days often include an extra-small, which would be impossibly tiny even for the average non-pregnant woman), and starving themselves after delivery, in order to get back to their 'normal' weight as soon as possible. Even that word, 'normal', is nuts. How can it be 'normal' to weigh the same, three weeks post-birth, as you did before conception?

Any kind of body weight issue has various and complex causes, mostly to do with stress, control and fear. However, a constant visual diet of Victoria Beckham and Heidi Klum with microscopic bumps and stick-thin arms right up to their due date, and then looking terrifyingly trim and toned six weeks post-partum, isn't helping. It may not make us anorexic, but it's definitely adding a layer of irritation and insecurity to the whole thing.

To Hell with Heat

The really funny/awful thing is that well-meaning friends so often give us copies of magazines like *Heat* and *Now* just after we've had a baby. They pop them in with the baby present and tub of hummus they've brought you. 'A little light reading,' they might say. A little light self-laceration, more like.

Of all the times to have to confront celebs looking fab post-baby (and there are *always* celebs looking fab post-baby in these magazines), this has to be the worst. There you are, feeling bulgy, sore, swollen, maybe leaking milk, almost certainly with a long streak of baby sick down your shoulder and wearing a faded tracksuit. Your house is a tip and you're an emotional wreck. This is not a good moment to see pictures of Rachel Zoe poured into a sleekly tailored black suit, with a mane of artfully tousled blonde hair and cerise lipstick, four weeks after giving birth. Nor will you want to read her insisting that 'I'm eating a ton and nursing my child. I have not exercised, I can tell you that much.'

Worse – much worse – are the celebs who look ten times better than you do who are *still* being chided by the magazine for not losing the baby weight or having hair like a bunch of twigs. Have you ever noticed how the magazines always cover this up by pretending they're 'celebrating' the curvier look of some poor celeb, congratulating her for 'proudly' baring her stomach or 'dressing down', except they've chosen to run the least flattering pic of this woman they can find? Sometimes they even draw a ring around the offending bit of flesh in case we've missed it.

In short, post-partum is not a good time to read these magazines. Do not be fooled into thinking they will 'inspire' you to make an effort with losing weight, the way some women put pictures of models in bikinis on their fridge doors as 'thinspiration'. This will not work. All that will happen is that you will feel worse about yourself, and then you'll reach for an extra chocolate biscuit.

The trouble is, even if you're a strong enough person to chuck the offending mags in the bin and wean yourself off your daily diet of online images, the rest of the world will continue to judge you with a grocer's eye for accuracy, and zero tolerance: 'Hmm, she had the baby over three months ago. Not bad, but really she should be a bit further along in getting her figure back...'

There's a window that operates here of roughly four to ten months. If you slim down earlier than four months, you're 'amazing'. Anything within the window is 'normal' and carries more muted approval, but find yourself still carrying weight after ten months, and you will start to feel the unspoken disapproval of everyone from other mums to the local butcher. These people will make judgements about your mental state – whether or not you're 'coping' – based on your appearance. They will start to feel sorry for your husband. Society *wants* you to be a Yummy Mummy, because in your groomed-and-glammed form you are more pleasant to look at, but also because Society doesn't like people to resist the norm. By not going along with what's expected, you find that you have opened a hornet's nest, thinking it was a beehive.

Right beside the idea of 'getting your figure back' is the ghostly spectre of 'letting yourself go'. And this one is unforgivable.

One Sexy Momma...

Like that joke of Dorothy Parker's – 'If all the young ladies who attended the Yale prom were laid end to end, no one would be the least surprised' – if there was indeed just *one* sexy momma, I wouldn't be in the least surprised. There can't be many more. Not new mommas, anyway.

Although you would be forgiven for thinking that half the world is At It within weeks of the birth, slipping back into their skinny jeans and raising hell in the bedroom. This is an extension of the Yummy Mummy, a kind of Triple XXX version hinted at by various Kardashians, and the result – whatever about the intention – is to make the rest of us feel appalling as we desperately try to think back to when the last time we had sex with our Significant Others was, and did that even count given that technically...

'Look Good, Feel Sexy, Get It On' goes the Mothershould mantra for this bit, tapping straight into a zone we're feeling pretty insecure about already. I firmly contend it is Not Normal to want to be rolling around in the hay for A Long Time after having a baby. I know there are some for whom the whole experience acts as a profound aphrodisiac – one friend who I visited a couple of days after the birth of her first baby said in tones of great indignation, 'I don't know why they won't let you have sex after the birth. I mean, if ever there was a time when you felt intimate and loving with your husband, that's it.' Apparently, she and said husband had been chased out of a toilet cubicle by an irate midwife.

I almost tripped over in my effort to get out of the house, immediately, and tell all our other friends what she had said.

That was back when the docs were on our side and forbade sex in the first six weeks post-birth. These days, they're disappointingly permissive about it, adopting a kind of 'when it feels right' approach that's very pressurising when, six months on, it still doesn't 'feel right'.

For ages, you bumble along in a world in which sex is of no more importance than world peace or Spring/Summer trends, or any of the other things you used to care passionately about. Then one day you look up for what feels like the first time in forever, and what do you see? A pregnant Victoria's Secret model on the runway! Beyoncé, who gave birth *months* later than you, wearing a tight salmon-pink ruched dress stretched over her magnificent curves, boobs falling out of the low-cut neckline! This is clearly a woman who is making Jay-Z very happy. So what the hell is wrong with you?

Nothing, actually. Because sex is the last thing most of us want with a small baby. It comes way, way below a decent night's sleep and ten minutes alone to read a book.

Face it, you just don't feel sexy with a flabby tummy, leaky, swollen boobs, mysterious internal pains, fuzzy hair (something weird happens to it post-birth; I remember growing prehistoric fronds from my forehead after one of the babies) and what feels like terminal exhaustion. And that's before we even get to the fundamental incompatibility between Madonna-with-Child and Sex Goddess. Perhaps the earth mother types get this one right, moving seamlessly from the nurturing of children to consciousness-expanding sexual intercourse, all an equal part of the great cycle of Gaia. I suspect that doesn't work for most of us.

Much is made of how unromantic and drudge-like life with small kids is – emptying potties, wiping noses, the smears of food – but I think most of us can put that behind us pretty easily. For me, the real passion-killer is the space-invading that goes on with children. They really don't get the exclusion zone thing. After a long day of being pressed up against, grabbed, held, hugged, stroked and kissed – all lovely, of course – my physical affection requirements have been well and truly met, and the last thing I feel like is more mauling. A vacuum seems quite appealing though.

Pick a Number and Double It

However, there's no point in pretending that sex isn't important. It is. Deep down, you know you should be making the effort. And this is the only *should* I will endorse, because yes, you should be. We all should be, if only so we can stop guilting over it. Domestic life gets even more grumpy and fraught if nothing is happening in the bedroom.

My tuppence worth? Just do it. Think of a number, double it, do it. If you think once a week is optimal, make it twice a week and go for it. If once a month is more your thing, aim for twice a month. Don't wait to be 'in the mood', because you may never be. It doesn't have to be tantric and mind blowing, but a bit of decent sex will work wonders for your overall mood and will stop that niggling worry at the back of your mind: '*How long* has it been…?'

It also means you can row properly about things without always feeling on the back foot because you're not putting out. The silent 'no sex' accusation wafting through the air is the unvoiced backdrop to many a domestic row.

It's like laundry really; just another chore to strike off the list. You can let it slide for a while, but leave it too long and the build-up starts to become alarming. And a decent shag will make you happy in a way that even loads of clean laundry will not. It will make your husband/partner happy in a way that an ironed shirt can't.

Anyway, why should Beyoncé have all the fun?

PART II
REBIRTH

Chapter 11

THE PAST IS ANOTHER COUNTRY (LITERALLY – IT'S BELGIUM)

In which I revisit my own childhood from the perspective of being a mother

None of us approaches having children alone. And I don't mean the person who is our biological partner in the venture. I mean the voices in our heads, the memories of our own childhoods.

These too form part of the chorus of *should*, even though they are usually more benign and at least have the virtue of having been real. But whether we want to replicate the exact circumstances of our own magical childhoods right down to the patterned tablecloth, do something radically different or anything in between, we can't ignore the power of this psychological landscape. Trying to is like being a cat with a tin can tied to its tail: the faster you run, the faster it drags along behind you.

How many of us have said something to a child without thinking, and then thought, 'God, I sound just like my mother'? Once we have children, the figures from our own childhood suddenly take on new life, putting on flesh in our recollections. We start to recall things we haven't thought about in years – certain looks; the feel of a hand on our arm, restraining or urging forward; that note of hysterical fear in a mother's voice as we walked too close to the edge or swung a sharp instrument at an irritating smaller child.

At the time, the hysterical note was a source of deep annoyance, triggering irrational rage at a level we didn't even know we had – I see this now in my own children, how angry they get when they hear it in my own voice. The memory of that annoyance is still there in the recesses of my own childhood, except that now, beside it, is a newly fitted out memory incorporating my own mother's point of view, like a fancy bit of camera work in a film flashback. Alongside my own irritation I can see her fear, her moment of terror at a near miss, the glancing blow of disaster that fell just outside the charmed circle. The shadow of what could have so awfully been that lay across the lighted path for a moment.

Now that we too carry that kernel of unrelenting fear in our hearts, we hear the hysterical note with sympathy. And we see, in hindsight, how very close our small selves actually were to the cliff edge or how narrowly our swipe missed the baby's eye. It is our business to see now, just as it was not our business to see then.

Having babies changes our perspective of the past for ever. But we need to hold the dual vision. There's no point going overboard with thinking, 'Oh, now I know what it was like for my mum.' We also need to remember what it was like for the children we were. Keep the two in mind and we're laughing, doubly armed for the battle to be our own sort of good mother.

The fragments of our own childhoods – misremembered, half-remembered, forgotten but absorbed – inevitably colour all our attempts to bring up children ourselves. They are the mood board of our psychology, the colour references and material swatches we turn to when trying to assemble a coherent response to the startling rabbit-from-a-hat trick that is having babies. My own background can seem a bit odd sometimes, but just as all dreams are really strange, everyone's childhood is extraordinary.

Welcome to My Psychological Hinterland...

My mother was born in Jerusalem and raised in Africa, soaking up the same expansive vision as the limitless skies of her childhood terrain. Brave, fierce, magnificent – she could be terrifying (truth be told, I'm still terrified of her), but was far more often kind.

She once charged at a boy with a pitchfork who had been chasing my brother and me when we were five and six, because he told her to 'feck off, Missus' when she ordered him off our garden wall. She had been digging the garden with the pitchfork; now she caught it up and ran for him, full tilt. He, in astonished fear, fell backwards off the wall into a waist-high thicket of nettles and ran off screaming.

'Now I know you really love me, Mummy,' my brother said.

My father's upbringing could seem much more dull; the brilliant only child of two Roscommon schoolteachers, he barely left the town before going to university at seventeen. But funnily, the physically limited surrounds of his childhood gave him the same kind of breadth of vision and expansive imagination. He was my hero from the time I was old enough to sit on his knee and eat his dinner (he got much more exciting food than we did). Of all the lovely things that were said and written about him after he died, the one that made the most sense to me was a quote from Yeats:

for your sole sake
Heaven has put away the stroke of her doom,
So great her portion in that peace you make
By merely walking in a room.

There was never a room I was in that didn't immediately shift on its molecular axis to become a more vibrant and reassuring place simply by the fact of his stepping into it.

These are the giants who stand at my shoulder while I try to work out how to bring up my own kids, who stand somewhere between me and the sun, casting their own, even brighter light. They inspire and caution me and I have enormous gratitude towards them. They're impossible acts to follow, but they give me every reason to try.

Mind that Child

By the time I was ten, we had moved house six times between Belfast, Dublin and Brussels. Each place we went, we seemed to acquire another baby. And that meant more responsibility for me. By the time I came to have children of my own, I knew exactly what to expect in terms of the relentlessness of it all. I had been trained up early. Other things surprised me, but the sheer volume of work was actually quite familiar.

'Emily, mind Francis!'

'Emily, mind Martha!'

'Emily, I told you to mind Baba.'

'Where was Emily? She was supposed to be minding him…'

There was a lot of minding that went on when I was growing up. I was second eldest, eldest girl, with three younger siblings – and then four younger siblings, because just when I thought it was all over, along came Baby Number Six.

I can remember the look on my best friend's face when she realised that my mother was having Another Baby. Her reaction was a mixture of pity and proper mortification. 'Your parents are still Doing It. Oh, god. What is everyone going to say?' We had boys in our class, teenage boys, so obsessed with sex that asking the French teacher what was the word for a seal (*un phoque*) could make them snigger for hours. With their collections of porn mags and hopeful attempts at spiking the drink of any girl who spoke to them for long enough with Spanish Fly (even though it was so lumpy, insoluble and chalk coloured that it would have required a great deal of honest goodwill to consume it at all), these boys spent their lives lost in dreams of someone, sometime, actually saying yes. And here I was, about to hand them a golden opportunity to publicly discuss the whole thing.

I knew exactly what they were going to say, and they did: 'Your parents have Done It at least six times.'

I was thirteen, my mother was forty-two. We lived in Brussels and went to the European School. Nobody had six children in their family. Nobody's mother was having another baby at the age of forty-two. And nobody had to mind their younger brothers and sisters like I did.

Few of my friends even had younger brothers or sisters. Or not that you'd notice. The few who did seemed allowed to treat their younger siblings any way they wanted. The law of primogeniture, in all its savage, elemental glory, was in operation. I didn't just have to mind my little siblings, keeping them safe and out of too much trouble – I had to be nice to them too. Our house had the opposite law to primogeniture: the youngest was always right.

There was one exception to the Youngest Is Always Right rule, and that was the Francis Is Always Right rule. He was fourth in line, with Martha behind him, so technically, in any incident involving her, he should have been the automatic fall guy. Except that he had the invisible but impregnable force field of my mother's protection drawn tight around him. Everything glanced off him, like jelly thrown against a window.

Because Francis was a sensitive child, full of insight and originality, but he was also very scratchy and wheezy. He had bad asthma and eczema almost from birth. Constant, low-lying itching and wheezing like a small train could give way to prolonged, intense bouts of both or either.

It was because of him that some of the more extreme rules of the household came into being. And because of him, these rules were not floutable. There could be no negotiation on the No Sugar and No TV rules, because both these things apparently Made Francis Wheeze, and preventing that was the primary mission of the entire household.

Calm, Cool, Consistent?

Consistency, like global warming, wasn't really a big deal back in the 70s and 80s. It certainly wasn't the Holy Grail of childrearing the way it is today. My parents definitely didn't much bother with it. They were certainly charismatic and brilliant, but consistent? Not so much.

Without it, a pretty simple system was in operation: if they were in a good mood, we had a good time; if they were in a bad mood, we got sent to bed.

Our rooms were at the very top of a tall house, full of wooden panelling and creaky stairs. The cheerful noise of downstairs gradually faded as you climbed, so that by the time you reached your room, you couldn't hear anything at all and might as well have been alone in the house. We hated being alone. We simply weren't used to it.

Upstairs was much colder than down and lacking in material comforts, because material comforts – carpets, curtains, cushions –

brought dust, and dust brought on asthma attacks. We had high ceilings and beautiful plasterwork, but bare boards and only what furniture was strictly functional. The best bit was that we had our own balcony, perfect for firing paper pellets or water balloons at passers-by on the street, and later, for smoking.

The problem with the lack of consistency was that there was no 'one minute per age of child' system in operation. Basically, you were stuck up there until you decided to come down and apologise. I was stubborn in many things, but when it came to this, I learned expediency very fast. I'd no sooner get upstairs than I would be shouting, 'I'm sorry. Can I come down now?'

I once told my father, years later, that I hadn't meant any of the apologies.

'Good,' he responded cheerfully. 'I didn't care if you meant it. The main thing was that you learned to say it.'

The visions from the past come at us adulterated by the ages. Distorted by time and the various mangles our own psychological needs have put them through, they can't really be trusted. People will always tell you, 'Well I was smacked/ left to scream for hours/ denied TV/ fed nuggets and chips, and I turned out fine.' But you can't entirely believe them.

Because who says they're fine? They do. And they undoubtedly believe it, and that's great. But who's to say they couldn't have been *even better* if they hadn't been smacked or fed Turkey Twizzlers? Unless they can present me with the results of a blind trial, involving an identical twin and carefully controlled circumstances that replicated their upbringing entirely but left out the Twizzlers or whatever it is they claim didn't do them any harm, then I cannot possibly be assured of their absolute fineness.

Neither can I be assured that my own childhood is as perfect as I recall. Even if I could, I'm not sure how much that helps. Ideally, I would cherry pick all the many wonderful bits from my childhood and replicate them, leaving out anything less than wonderful. But it doesn't work like that. It's a package, this whole dip-into-the-past thing, and it's far from infallible.

The urge to make comparisons with something bathed in the golden glow of nostalgia and make it Time Regained is a strong one, but a useless one. And so I have a duty to remember just how irritating being sent upstairs was, even as I try so hard to recreate the teas of homemade apricot jam on toast and games of murder in the dark.

Tears of a Clown

One of our au pairs, taking pity on our spartan surroundings, once bought us two framed paintings, one for the boys' bedroom, one for the girls'. The boys' was a sad clown sitting against a wall in an attitude of floppy dejection, ruffled cuffs falling over his limp hands, tragic eyes fixed imploringly on the viewer. We girls got a boy and girl with enormous eyes, holding hands, heading down a train track. A pair of adorable rogues in ostentatiously darned and patched clothes. I think He might have been trying to steal a kiss while She coyly ducked away.

We were ecstatic. Nothing so elegant could have been imagined. We couldn't wait to show our parents.

'Mummy, look what Esmé bought us!'

'Oh dear. You can't put that up.'

'But Mummy!'

The pictures went into Esmé's bedroom, not ours, to join her china Pierrot and Harlequin dolls and the Champagne cork with the 50p piece in it from her 18th birthday, and we were left to try to salvage elegance from wherever we could.

I had a Pierrot doll too, but mine was antique and immensely fragile, and almost macabre in its silent porcelain eloquence, with its smooth painted cap and cobwebby lace ruff. Not robustly jolly like Esmé's, with its white and black satin romper suit and a felt cap. You couldn't cuddle my Pierrot doll.

We did have a playroom full of dolls, but they were feral – wild-haired from washing, scribbled over with biro for make-up, wearing old dusters and raggedy babygros handed down from several children before they reached the dolls. We used to think they could come alive and would try to sneak up to catch them at play. Actually, I'd say they might have tried to kill us. Being left alone with them once evening had fallen was an unnerving experience.

Limitlessly kind to those in real need, sentimentality was worse than gunrunning in my mother's book. Birthdays fell into the category of sentimental, so we didn't much bother with them after the age of six or seven. And as for Mother's Day, don't get her started…

Gifts in general were viewed with dampened enthusiasm. For my confirmation, my best friend, Elizabeth, came to the house and presented me with a can of Impulse she had bought me. She was Protestant and didn't have confirmation in the same way we did, but she knew it was a big deal and had gifted accordingly.

I sprayed myself liberally with Delightfully Daring and ran down, Elizabeth at my heels, to show my mother. Now, I wasn't a total idiot – I had a fair idea that I needed to explain that the Impulse was a present before my mother saw it and decided to throw it out – so my running down was pre-emptive as much as it was demonstrative. But I hadn't reckoned on my mother's notorious sense of smell (a real curse in the years when I started smoking). No sooner had we entered her bedroom than she called from her bathroom, 'Emily, what is that horrible smell of cheap perfume?'

Crestfallen and mortified, I answered, 'It's the perfume Elizabeth gave me for my confirmation.'

My mother had the grace to be a little embarrassed, and Elizabeth, who really was a trooper, said cheerfully, 'It's all right. It *was* cheap.'

Once, after a row, I forced my brothers and sisters to give me their money and bought a big bunch of flowers for my mother to say sorry. 'Oh. Just like one of the au pairs,' she said weakly.

For years I parroted this faintly mocking line about presents, even taking a slightly perverse pride in celebrating my birthday precisely between the hours of 3.15 and 3.35 pm each December 23rd – just long enough for my mother to suggest cutting the Christmas cake 'because it's Emily's birthday', for my sister to say 'no, you can't cut the cake, it's for Christmas' and everyone else to go 'oh right, it's your birthday; happy birthday'. Not a minute's more birthday celebrations were encouraged. But then I married a man whose family celebrates every birthday like it's Armistice Day, and had children who seemed similarly inclined towards extravaganza. Something had to give. In the end, it was my curmudgeonly nature. My mother's indifference to presents and the making of fusses is genuine; mine was a bit of a sham.

Last Mother's Day, my children bought me a gift set of Suddenly Madame Glamour shower gel and moisturiser, from Lidl. I nearly wept with the sheer beauty of it.

Among Us, Not of Us

The au pairs. A horde of them tramps though my memory. Many are faceless, nameless, characterless at this distance, but some stand out. There was Fat Sarah, Thick Sarah and the Scottish one who ran away with a North African man in the middle of the night and left a note asking my mother to tell her parents. The bubbly Irish twins who I could never tell apart. A pretty English girl who was devastated to discover we weren't more like the Von Trapps (six children, you see – I suspect my mother subtly traded on this in adverts), spent a week running up our phone bill while she wept to her parents back home, then departed with a promise to refund the airline ticket and phone bill and never did. There was the beautiful

Ingrid who stayed for years and was adored by all of us; Anne from Northern Ireland, with a mop of thick black curls and who was great fun. Then in later years a stream of Danish girls – Penella, who made amazing pizza and never bothered speaking to us, and one whose name I don't remember who took me to the police station to translate for a friend of hers who had been involved in a date rape. I was about fifteen at the time. My parents, when they came home, felt just as you might expect about this.

Some left no impression at all; others gave me a blueprint for what being grown up might be like: boyfriends, nightclubs, bottles of Champagne sent over by mysterious men. A couple of them were decent and would take me into town, buy me the odd beer once I reached fifteen (sixteen is legal for pubs in Belgium) and allow me to go into school the next day, boasting. They were part of our lives in the same sort of way the cats were: among us, but not of us.

Into the Jungle

Because we lived in Brussels, we had no extended family – no cousins, uncles, grandparents – to take some of the heat off the pressure cooker that is any family life.

Actually, we were low on extended family anyway – my father was an only child, his father died when I was a year old and his mother ('Old Granny', as we called her) lived with us on and off in various houses in Dublin and Brussels, but never with huge success.

A former Roscommon town schoolteacher of formidable reputation and intellect, she clearly (rightly) thought we were a wild, unruly bunch and tried to counteract this by grabbing us with a skinny hand as we ran past, whooping and chasing each other, and putting us through our paces in Irish. This was really no good, because our Irish was very bad, what with living away from the country, and anyway we considered it an outrage to be asked questions of such a clearly academic nature outside the confines of school. Seen through her eyes – and occasionally I caught a quick, shaming glimpse – we were rough, noisy and unmannerly. The very opposite of the thoughtful, precocious child she had raised. Our good qualities, such as they were, were hard to demonstrate to her because we never stayed still long enough.

My mother had one brother and he had two children, our only first cousins. They were lovely, but many years younger than us, and in a different country, so there was really very little outside interference. We were like one of those tribes discovered in the jungle who have evolved strange customs and a language all their own.

In the absence of relatives, we had a few very close family friends who had kids roughly our age. They took the place of cousins and were the extended family we otherwise lacked. We were lucky because the children in these families shared our love of adventure and other people's gardens. And because, being Irish, they understood the rules about Minding Children. Just as well, because local Belgian kids wouldn't play with us.

'Can Solange Come Out and Play?'

We tried at first, full of cheerful certainty. We knocked on the door of a girl who lived across the street who we had been formally – very formally – introduced to a few days earlier, and summoned up our scant reserves of French.

'Can Solange come out and play?' we asked her mother.

Stunned silence.

'*Ou est-ce vous jouez?*' Where are you playing?

'*Dans la rue, mais pas dans le trafic.*' In the street, but not in the traffic.

She looked puzzled. The vulgarity of playing in the street was clearly no worse than the danger of playing in the traffic.

'Ah … one minute. Um, please come in. I'll see if she has finished her homework.'

Now, it was not the Done Thing to invite the soliciting children in. You didn't do that. You left them on the doorstep, sometimes even shut the door in their faces, and yelled for your child, who then shot out of the house like a stone from a slingshot. Or at least such was the way we had learned from our few years living in an estate in Dublin, pre-Brussels, where all the kids on the road played outside until dark every evening. They rang, they asked, they waited, you went out when you could.

And now this woman was asking us in, making us stand on a mat in the hallway – she wasn't quite mad enough to let us in any further with those muddy shoes on – while she went to 'see'.

We heard a whispered consultation between her and Solange that went on for ages. They were clearly trying to come up with a plan to counteract the shock of our unexpected request. It began to dawn on us that perhaps Belgian children didn't 'play out'.

She returned. Solange hadn't finished her homework, but if we would like to take off our shoes and sit 'there' – indicating a neat sofa by the window – she would come to us as soon as she could. We could look at a picture book while we waited. My younger brothers and sisters shifted miserably behind me. Were we going to be trapped now? It was all up to me.

'No, thank you. We will return to outside and maybe Solange she can come when she is ready.'

'Yes, of course.'

She never did.

From there, we worked it out pretty fast. Belgian children didn't play out. They played at home, or organised rather formal playdates that involved a lot of questions from Maman about how were we liking Brussels (a lot) and how was our French coming along (badly). They certainly never ran screaming round the place or broke into other people's gardens by scaling the network of red-tiled walls that ran into each other, making smooth, accessible paths for crawling along, before dropping a manageable distance onto a compost heap or shinning down a pear tree. What fun there was, we were going to have to get it ourselves.

Adventures in Wonderland

Brussels was a good place for this. Unmarked territory. Because the little Belgian children stayed in their houses or were escorted sedately to and from lessons, we felt like we had the run of the place. Empty streets, empty gardens, old people with tiny dogs, all under a flat grey-white sky.

Culturally, we were far more like the Moroccan kids than Belgians. They too had big families, where children of many ages hung out together, eldest responsible for youngest and everyone under instructions to get out and stay out. They stripped off and splashed in the park fountains just as we did, as no well-brought-up Belgian child ever would have done. They played wild games, yelled, wrestled each other and instantly closed ranks against outsiders.

They might have been more similarly minded, but they didn't much like us either. Instead of making friends, we fought; sometimes just jeering, other times proper punching.

With our scruffy clothes and mops of dark hair, we even looked quite North African (to our immense pride), at least to the hostile eyes of Belgian shopkeepers and officials.

'*Vous etes Maroccains?*' Chilly demeanour.

'*Non, Irlandais.*'

'*Nerlandais?*' A shade of warmth would creep into the voice.

'*Non, Irlandais. Irlande.*'

'*Ah, Irlandais!*' Cue lots of warmth, maybe even some back-slapping, usually followed by a thumbs up and, depending on their age and inclination, '*Irlande. L'IRA, oui?*' Or '*Irlande. U2, oui? Sunday, Bluuudy Sunday?*'

Once they knew we were Irish, they liked us a whole lot more.

The Magic Circle

In comparison, my children have such a dull life. Or they do at the moment. Presumably their teenage years may change and challenge all that, but just now, they seem to never be without parental supervision, accompanied to and from school, activities and playdates. I always know where they are, and if they disappear from my sight momentarily, I immediately begin to panic and presume they've been snatched.

As a result, they're like dogs with those collars that sound a high-pitched note when the perimeter is breached – inaudible to us, deeply unpleasant to them. They are self-regulating in their quest for freedom, conditioned to stay close and ask permission. I think they would be just as disturbed to find themselves completely without adult supervision as I would be to find them thus. Which seems awful – tame, restricted, with none of the rush of glorious freedom that we knew.

I don't think I'm alone in thinking this. Don't many of us consider with regret the different, tamer lives our children lead? It's not because I lived in Belgium that my childhood was so untrammelled; it's the era I grew up in, not the location. These days, all children have limited freedom and adventure in comparison with their parents' upbringing. There's a whole general level of guilt about this, even though we can't possibly do anything about it.

The landscape of my childhood seems wild and exciting when I look back now and compare it with the daily realities of my children's lives. An intoxicating time of freedom and discovery. But I suspect that's just childhood, the simple drama of growing up, regardless of the staging. In which case, we can relax.

If it's childhood itself that holds all the magic (and 'magic', of course, can be good and bad), then we can, with a big sigh of relief, stop agonising over our kids' curtailed physical freedom and accept that their experiences, though different, are equally as intense.

Because in comparison with, say, my mother's childhood – Africa, basically; Kenya and Tanzania – ours was pretty dull. No wild animals, no guns, no diamond mines. But we had something she didn't: we had each other. A big family, close in age and close in interests. My mother, with just one younger brother and too many changes of house and school, longed for more siblings.

And my children have things I didn't. People are nice to them, with the cheerful kindness the Irish generally show to children. No strangers were nice to us when we were young. They were suspicious and presumed we were up to no good, and if we didn't understand them, they shouted at us. Sometimes they slapped us – my youngest sister was once dealt a stinging whack on her fat bare leg in church when she was about two by an old man incensed by the way she was running up and down the aisle.

We were nagged, suspected, accused of everything from littering to pilfering, and once of breaking a swing. That time, the police were called and transported us round the corner to our house in a van, threatening to take us down to the station and lock us up if we didn't stop crying.

Shopkeepers invariably ignored us and served the lady behind us, and if we dared to protest, the whole shop would join in a chorus of how rude we were and where did we say we were from?

My children understand what's going on around them, which must make life a far more sensible place. We mostly didn't have a clue what was going on. Even when we learned French, we entirely missed the cultural subtleties. As a result, we mostly switched off – unless it directly and immediately affected us, it wasn't worth paying attention to. Yes, we were privileged to grow up in a different country, to learn another language and different customs, but the price we paid was social disconnection. We perched on the surface of Belgium, never getting any deeper than the obvious. We had no Belgian friends, no entry into real Belgian life.

If we went out as a family, together, we were supposed to behave extra well because of the natural hostility of any Belgian restaurateur who saw us coming. Of course that was impossible, so we were always conscious of disapproving looks and sly, derogatory comments.

My children have team sports, which they love and which make up a big part of their lives. These things were open to us as an option in Brussels, but you try getting really stuck into a hockey team made up of a load of Belgian girls who believe themselves to be innately superior and are as curious about other lives as a rabbit about a stone. Bridget and I were the worst players, on the worst team, in the worst league. No fun there.

My children belong to a community. They have cousins and friends close by, a world that is interested in them. They are connected in a way I never was. And this will have to do them in place of my experience of the intoxicating freedom of being Lord Of All I Surveyed, and utterly dispensable to the wider world I lived in.

Chapter 12

IT'S PURE POISON

In which I realise that Wilde was wrong when he said all women become their mothers – I haven't, but maybe I should try to

Growing up, it sometimes seemed like everything in our lives was a substitution. Where other families had peanut butter, we had tahini. They had chocolate, we had carob. They had sugar, we had honey. They had toffee bars, we had liquorice bars. They had jelly – ooh, we had jelly too! But it was made from carrageen moss sweetened with agave syrup. An entire culinary parallel universe – not Willy Wonka, more like Willy Wonky.

My older brother's seventh birthday. The table is a sea of good things. They are not the sorts of good things any of the children at the party have seen before. Dried apricots, raisins, apples, fat Medjool dates, thick-cut brown bread ham-and-cheese sandwiches, some with great rings of raw onion thrown in. Nuts galore – Brazil, hazel, almond. Not peanuts though, because apparently the Masai don't eat peanuts and so we must be suspicious of them. And certainly not dry-roasted, salted peanuts. It might be a birthday, but we're not going to go crazy here.

'Could you pass me that plate of chocolate biscuits?' My sister Bridget looked down the line of the boy's arm to where he was pointing, thinking to herself, 'Chocolate biscuits? That doesn't sound very likely.'

'Those are dried figs,' she explained once her eye had come to rest on the object of his desire.

'Oh, no thanks then,' he responded politely, dejected.

The plates of dates, nuts, figs and apricots were left largely untouched. I could see the children were all pinning their hopes on the cake. I mean, what could be wrong with cake? they were probably thinking. Clearly none of them had ever heard of carrot cake.

Actually, it wasn't carrot cake. It was a Victoria sponge, made with whole-wheat flour and as little Demerara sugar as it is possible to put into something and still call it 'cake' rather than simply 'bread in a cake shape'. It was thinly iced with a dusting of sugar dissolved in lemon juice. No colouring, no sugar flowers, no hundreds and thousands. As plain as the host of the Plymouth Brethren. To us, it was utterly delicious, but I could see that it was ashes in the mouths of these children raised on refined flour and sugar.

And this was the 1970s. That glorious era of Technicolor food, before the spoilsports got involved with their talk of childhood obesity, diabetes and ADHD. I have friends who even now can go into a reverie about the sweets of their childhood, names tripping off their tongues like memories of past lovers: Black Jacks, flying saucers, liquorice torpedoes, space dust, sherbet fountains, candy cigarettes.

Most of this stuff has been discontinued – too packed full of artificial flavouring and E-numbers to survive regulation – but the memories live on in the minds of those who grew up on it. The cultural and culinary landscape of my youth bears no resemblance to that of my friends. My family and I might as well have been living in the 1940s or 50s for all the impact the 70s had on us. And when, in the 1980s, I tried to orchestrate enough teenage rebellion to actually meet the 80s halfway, well, I'd say the Red Sea parted with greater ease.

When it came to food, my mother was so far ahead of her time that she was perched on the very edge of the lunatic fringe, staring happily into an abyss that would shortly be filled with organic, biodynamic, holistic and earth-friendly practices. Back then, though, she was almost alone in believing sugar and white flour to be the work of the devil. What sympathisers and fellow travellers she had were few and far between in the expat and Eurocrat circles of Brussels. They had retired to places like Donegal and Orkney, the better to live lives of unadulterated purity. I wonder if their kids stuck out as conspicuously as we did?

'If You're Hungry, You'll Eat It'

If any of those children at the birthday party had opened our kitchen cupboards, they would have seen wholegrain rice, whole-wheat spaghetti, bread so brown and coarse you'd think it was made from sawdust. Oh, and nothing in *packets*. No pretty pictures of smiling people consuming the products. Because our food didn't come from places where anybody bothered with such things. It was all homemade, homespun, slabs hewn from even bigger slabs and wrapped in plain brown paper. The ham was carved off the bone by the butcher. The cheese came from a huge wheel in the cheese-mongers. There were no cute, grinning boys and girls deployed to persuade consumers that their version of the ham-or-cheese world was the most desirable. The insides of those cupboards showed a vision of austerity that could have been war related, or post-nuclear. I used to look through the cupboards in my friends' houses just for the sheer joy of seeing brightly coloured packaging, something that made an effort to *seduce* me, rather than sitting there saying 'if you're hungry, you will eat me happily', which was more or less what my mother used to say when we said, 'I'm hungry!'

'There's some brown rice in the fridge, you could heat it up with a bit of miso.'

'I'm not hungry for *that* kind of thing.'

'Well, then, you can't really be hungry.'

Yoghurt came in glass jars without much in the way of adornment. These jars could be washed, returned and refilled with *Lactobacillus* cultures. No one had then heard the word 'live' for yoghurt. Music, maybe. Or wires. Not stuff you ate. Certainly it wasn't a 'good' thing the way it is now. It was hippy. And not very tasty, because the hippies allowed the 'natural sugar' of the fruit to sweeten the yoghurt. In the 70s and 80s, anything without an immense dollop of refined sugar was pretty much considered inedible.

Cooking in our house happened in huge iron pots and pans, impossible to clean and heavy with the black of ages. And everything was made from scratch. 'Where do you keep your stock cubes?' a helpful friend asked when we were whipping up a pan of spag bol one day.

'Stock cubes?' I'd never heard of such a thing. In our house, stock was made with the bones of whatever fowl had most recently been consumed and boiled for hours until it reduced to a thick viscousness, becoming the source of much gloating over its excellent richness and goodness.

The rules about sugar followed us outside the house, to the houses of our friends, to picnics, to what might be called Family Fun Days now, but were just days out then. My mother dreaded those like I imagine a lemming mother might dread trips to the seaside.

We, however, were shameless.

There was a delicate art to this. Get it right, and we might be able to cram in a few custard creams and cups of fizzy pop. (We ate sweet things like addicts, in haste and secretly, like the French are said to eat ortolans, those tiny birds they drown in brandy, behind their napkins, to hide their shame from God. I know that feeling.) Get it wrong though – be too greedy, too obvious – and we risked being simply snatched up and taken home, like lambs lifted by eagles.

Our best insurance – and well we knew it – was to get someone else on my poor mother's case, a champion for our cause. 'Oh Pat, let them. Just this once. It's not going to *kill* them.' The thing is, my mother truly believed that it was going to kill us. Maybe not immediately, in a dramatic, foaming-at-the-mouth-and-shaking sort of way, but eventually, inexorably and with much misery to be endured beforehand. In our house, we were told that Elvis died from an excess of hamburgers and Coca-Cola, rather than the more conventional explanation – an overdose of prescription drugs.

But it had to be the right champion. The wrong one – women who were actually infuriated by my mother's intransigence and were therefore less champions than covert sneerers – could ruin everything. Because my mother, who had the courage of a lion in everything, certainly had it when it came to her convictions. If the picnic or whatever else was seriously threatening her vision of what was right – or making Francis wheeze – she thought nothing of simply bundling all of us back into the car and leaving. And because she couldn't drive, that meant my father had to come too.

'Liam, we're leaving.'

He never seemed to mind. When it came to bringing up children, he did not dispute my mother's dominion or her excellence. Even though, I couldn't help feeling sometimes, he might have wished we were all a little more … normal. Especially when he encountered us running around the streets with dirty bare feet in our pyjamas.

What's a Mango?

Other children's birthday parties would often be preceded by a phone call from my mother to the mother of the birthday girl.

'Emily will be bringing her own sandwiches. She can have a slice of birthday cake, but nothing else.' And so I would sit, sometimes with my sister Bridget, sometimes alone, with thick doorsteps of bread and rough-hewn cheese like something Michelangelo might have worked from, while the rest of the party opened their mouths and mindlessly swallowed tablefuls of sugary treats like so much plankton. They didn't even know how lucky they were. They got this stuff all the time.

Sometimes I think about the birthday mothers and how they must have felt, effectively being told by my mother, 'You feed your kids crap, and that is your own affair, but *my* daughter is not to be allowed to eat such rubbish.' I think they felt sorry for me, but they never cheated the way I hoped they might. Occasionally I would detect a shade of something frosty in their demeanour, a touch less of the effusiveness they were busily forcing in their dealings with the other children. But they never disobeyed orders and slipped me an extra slice or a secret bun. I'd say it was fear of my mother rather than any agreement with her beliefs that stopped them.

What did astonish me was the readiness of other kids to police a situation that had nothing at all to do with them.

'You're not allowed that,' I'd be told, loudly, by some small girl, ostensibly my friend, as I tried to sneak a Rice Krispie bun under cover of the general chaos.

'*Mum*, Emily's taking a bun. She's not *allowed*.'

I know much more about the Stanford prison experiment now than I did then, so I get their psychological need to identify with the System much better. At the time I thought they were just being little busybodies. Oh wait, they *were* just being little busybodies.

'What's that?' Kids pointing at our lunchboxes was a common occurrence.

'A mango.'

'A rice cake.'

'Baked apple.'

'Honeycomb.'

'Weirdo.'

This was generally said with affection. And in fact, there are many highly functioning adults today who had their first taste of exotic fruit and sugar-substitutes thanks to the contents of my lunchbox back in 1980-whatever. One friend, James, still recalls the first time he ever saw a lychee.

'I thought it was a raw animal heart. Then you peeled it and I saw it was a dead baby bird…'

Some of them even swapped, eagerly. Not half as eagerly as me.

Oh, how I envied them their thin white-bread sandwiches with a sliver of ham inside, the pale processed pink of a kitten's tongue. Sandwiches that dissolved to nothing in the mouth – not like mine, which required vigorous chewing. As for the ones who got Pot Noodle for lunch … bliss!

My ideal lunch would have been one of the thin white-bread sandwiches, maybe with a slice of processed cheese in it, an apple and a packet of crisps. So discreet, so neat (our bread made such huge crumbs, and had such thick crusts). So normal. Sigh.

Offered a death row meal, anything at all I wanted, aged ten, I would have asked for tinned spaghetti hoops, or maybe tinned ravioli. With frozen chips.

The result of my mother's vigilance is that we were *obsessed* with sweets. No crack addict has ever thought about their fix as intensely as we did about sweets. We used to draw pictures of fantasy birthday parties, tables groaning under the weight of jellies, cakes, iced buns, jugs of lemonade, plates of chocolate biscuits, éclairs, meringue with whipped cream, tubs of chocolate chip ice cream…

We were perfectly happy to eat sugar in any form it presented itself in, including joke shop sweets filled with pepper. Seriously.

We picked up chewing gum from the ground and ate it, until even we realised that this was pretty disgusting (it was all the rage in Dublin housing estates in the 1970s, but did not travel well, as a concept, to Brussels). After my parents' dinner parties, we crept downstairs at dawn to raid the leftovers. Puddles of melted home-made coffee ice cream were fine with us, as were the half-eaten ingots of Gianduja that my mother bought from Godiva, even when lightly covered in cigar ash – we just dusted it off. Whatever remained added a faint, pleasant flavour and grit to the chocolate hazelnut paste.

After mass at St Anthony's church, place of worship for the Irish community in Brussels, light refreshments were served in the parish hall opposite. It was the kind of conviviality expat communities go in for, our version of gin and tonics on the porch of the Muthaiga Country Club in Nairobi.

We badgered my parents to go there, rather than the local Belgian church they much preferred, because if we got on our marks and ran the very second that 'go, the mass is ended' was followed by 'thanks be to God', we could reach the parish hall and throw back a couple of cups of Fanta, followed by some stale digestives, before my father caught up with us. My mother didn't go to mass. Not there, anyway, even though, having been schooled by Loreto nuns in Kenya, she was deeply religious in a ritualistic kind of way. Anything remotely folksy wounded her aesthetic sensibilities, so she mostly gave church a miss, communing with her own God in cathedrals and woods.

We talked about sweets with all the inventiveness of artists, dreaming up our perfect, magical combinations, decorating them with hundreds and thousands, sugar roses and sprinkles galore. We stole pennies any chance we got and spent them on the cheapest sweets the corner shop had to offer, until my mother asked the shopkeeper not to serve us.

Asking a Belgian to refrain from commercial activity is like asking a bee not to buzz. Not even my mother could get that one across the line.

'I Hate That!'

These days, as I find myself cooking three meals a night and making endless concessions to the food foibles of my children, I admire my mother's complete lack of compromise more than ever. The magnificence with which she served up cabbage leaves rolled into cigar shapes, filled with chopped lamb, rice and herbs, or boeuf bourguignon to which pigs trotters had been added for extra succulence and richness, to loud choruses of 'I HATE THAT, I'm not eating it', leaves me stunned with admiration.

With her implacable vigilance in mind, I am horrified to conduct a spot check on the contents of my kitchen cupboards: peanut butter (no added salt or sugar, but *still* ... the Masai!), white rice, chocolate biscuits, white bread, Jelly Tots (that's a bit of an aberration, they came from a party bag), cooking chocolate. I even have an emergency supply of oven chips.

As for how that makes me feel? Like a birth traitor, since you ask.

I used to be much stricter about this stuff. My eldest child didn't see a sweet until he was nearly three. He thought raisins were a treat and that all muffins came with giant bits of carrot and apple sticking out of them. I have a friend with a son slightly older than mine. Until very recently, she made up a separate going-home bag for my little boy after her son's birthday party. Instead of jellies and Smarties, he got raisins and one of those tubes of dried fruit.

But once he was old enough to notice what other kids had that he didn't, I just didn't have the heart to deny him, or the stomach for the fight. Too many memories of parties at which I stared so wistfully at the other kids cramming in sugar in all its forms.

The wall came tumbling down gradually. First it was birthday parties and other Extra-Ordinary occurrences. Then we slipped into the odd treat at home, maybe on a Sunday. That soon became every Sunday and sometimes a Wednesday too. Now, my children believe it is their divine right to be rewarded with a biscuit or similar (there is a very complicated system of equivalences that goes on – a piece of chocolate, although smaller than a biscuit, is worth the same because it is rarer; a plain biscuit (rich tea) is worth less than a chocolate one, and so on) on a daily basis.

'What's for dessert?' they cheerfully ask, deaf to my boring tales of how 'in my day we never...', except from an anthropological point of view, a curiosity as to How The World Used To Work.

And even though I am way more tolerant of 'pure poison' than they have any right to expect, they still conduct Halloween trick-or-treating like a black op: stealthy, speedy, secretive. At no point do they allow me to see their swag-bag in case I say, 'Right, that's more than enough, let's go home.' Or worse, 'You can't eat *that*.'

And even though they sleep with the bags under their beds, I still tiptoe in and cull the really bad stuff – the hysterically coloured and E-numbered stuff – before they have had time to memorise the contents.

The question of who will eat what at mealtimes is one I expend way too much energy on. My system for dealing with food refusal vacillates wildly between feigned indifference ('fine, eat what you want'), on the basis that this is apparently the 'best' way to deal with the matter, to phased disciplinary procedures ('don't eat if you don't want, but you won't get any dessert'), through to complete over-reaction ('if you don't eat *everything* on your plate, you can go straight to bed!').

Apparently, we are supposed to ignore all 'dislikes' and continue to offer the food at intervals, on the basis that tastes change and one day they might shout, 'Brilliant! Broccoli!' instead of falling to the floor in despair at the sight of green spears.

But I don't. I really can't stand the miserable poking at little bits of green stuff, or the hysterical accusation, 'It's got *onion*!' Instead, I adapt the meal to accommodate different tastes, even making allowances for the one who doesn't like things to touch and who won't eat his roast potatoes if they have been 'ruined' by a brush with his roast lamb.

This means that on a night when chicken is the main offering, this can appear in three or four different ways: grilled chicken breast for me, roast drumsticks for two of the kids, homemade nuggets for the really fussy one and a combination of everything for my husband.

I know I'm not supposed to do this, but who has the energy for nightly battles about food? Followed, in extreme cases, by a child going to bed hungry because you have both been inflexible? On the basis that I know plenty of adults who claim to have been hysterically picky eaters and are now grand with all but a few pet hates (sprouts, generally, and parsnip), and in recollection of the few but pointless occasions in my own childhood where someone (usually my older brother) was left sitting at the table until he finished his turnip (I mostly finished it for him; I love turnip), I am happy to compromise.

But somewhere inside me, the rules of my childhood are still sacred. In comparison to my mother, I'm so relaxed about refined sugar and flour as to be positively Grateful Dead-like. Yet I'm still capable of feeling that a whole day has been ruined if, as so often happens, following a walk or trip to the playground with other families someone utters the fatal words, 'Let's get hot chocolates.' Or worse again, 'Let's get ice cream.'

I twitch spasmodically, involuntarily. 'Why can't we all just have fun and then simply *go home*?' I think to myself. 'Why this need to cap the perfectly lovely day by ingesting high fructose corn syrup in all its deadly forms? Why are people so bloody *greedy*?'

This is my mother's voice speaking through me. Not that she would say 'bloody'. And she would say it loud and clear for all to hear, not mutter it to herself, like I do.

As for waiters in restaurants... I know people complain that they can be unwelcoming to children. My problem is the exact opposite. They are much too nice.

'Who's for ice cream?' they roar as they clear plates, without so much as an interrogatory raised eyebrow in my direction. Bravo, waiter. Thanks! You've just handed my children a gun, which they will lose no time in putting to my head: 'Yes! Please, can we have ice cream? Can we? Please? Please?' Cue either a nasty battle or weary capitulation.

My friends don't feel at all the same way (I heard one of them sending her daughter into a house where some of us were staying for Easter with the merrily malicious instruction, 'Make sure you *share* your sweets. Especially with Emily's kids!'), but in these days of alterno-lifestyles and heightened awareness over diet, I'm far less of an oddity than my mother was.

Even the local football team my elder son plays for takes it in good part when I give out about the casual way in which they shower 'juice drinks' (the work of the devil, in particularly sneaky form), full-size chocolate bars and other unnecessary 'treats' on the players.

'Lost a game? Don't worry, have a juice drink and a packet of jellies.'

'Won the league? Well done, have a can of Coke and a Mars bar.'

They think I'm a bit mad – you know, kind of dotty but well meaning, with a crazy bee in my bonnet, someone who can be indulged without actually being listened to. And I, to my shame, allow them to believe this. I am not enough my mother's daughter. She would have come to every match armed with apples, a carob bar and utter indifference to public opinion.

For me, food is not just food. Perhaps it never is for any of us. It's another sphere in which I feel I *should* be doing better than I am.

All that baggage from my childhood combined with the new focus we all need to have on what our kids eat (childhood obesity, remember?) creates something of a toxic mess.

This is the topic in which I have to try hardest not to be judgemental. When I see other mothers handing out Smarties to their kids like, well, like Smarties, I twitch with the urge to say, 'You're killing them! That stuff is pure poison!' See how easy it is to turn into one of the Shoulderati?

So why not just say it? After all, Society is behind me all the way on this one. The Shoulderati go into overdrive on the need for nutritious meals, busily fostering the all-out war going on between mothers who cook from scratch and those who defrost. Giving your kids stuff someone else made in a factory, rather than made by your own fair hands (or hands you have hired) from natural, organic ingredients, is the clearest way in which you can now be a 'bad' mother in the eyes of your peers.

It's too easy, that's why. And the target is always wrong. The mothers who know it's bad but don't mind just this once (or twice) don't need me to tell them. And the mothers who don't know need far more than me ranting at them.

The Good Food vs. Bad Food debate is Society at its most patronising and judgemental: 'Here are some food stamps to feed your family, Ms Mother, but you're not allowed to use them on sugary drinks or processed meals because those are bad for you.' It's an attitude I fundamentally agree with, but it still makes me cringe to see it in practice. If Society is so keen to improve the eating habits of the poor (it's basically the poor we're talking about here), then Society should tackle the big food corporations, not browbeat mothers who have limited options and education.

It matters what we feed them – a lot – but other things matter just as much or more, and the spectacle of Society queuing up to judge mothers on their skills in the kitchen is just as revolting as burgers full of horse meat.

Chapter 13

DID YOU SEE *EASTENDERS* LAST NIGHT?

In which I trawl the lessons of my childhood for guidance

'Did you see *EastEnders* last night?' Words to strike terror into my heart. It could have been *Top of the Pops*, or that soothingly bland show with Esther Rantzen where she examined consumer rights, or any of the other programmes considered mandatory viewing by my school friends. Whatever it was, the answer was always going to be no.

We weren't allowed to watch TV.

Exceptions were made for *Rentaghost* on Wednesday afternoons, because we had a half-day then, and *The A-Team* on Saturday night. Everything else was considered unsuitable and unnecessary. There was a brief period where we got *Grange Hill* (a gritty BBC school drama) in under the radar, but then I shouted something like 'I didn't ask to be born' at my mother during an argument and she decided that was me 'acting out' the kind of 'low-class' TV I'd been watching – apparently I even said it in an English accent – so that was the end of *Grange Hill* for the entire family, who of course were furious.

'It rots your brain.'

'Children should be outside, playing, not cooped up in front of the TV.'

'It makes Francis wheeze.'

Game over.

My mother may well have been right (though I'm not sure there's an established connection between watching TV and child-hood asthma), but what good was that to me at an age when no one has any conversation except 'did you see...?'

This was pre-teenage years, so pre- 'who fancies who' and 'who snogged who'. Now that half the class no longer ran around pretending to be horses while the other half pretended to groom and feed the horses, TV was all we had. The tangled plot lines of various soap operas, the who-did-what of game show contestants were the stuff of schoolyard conversation. Except that my family and I didn't have it.

What we did have was one very valuable window of opportunity in the morning, when the school bus collected us and allowed us twenty precious minutes in which to get to work.

No MI5 interrogator was ever as skilful or stealthy as my sister Bridget and I at dissembling, at leading witnesses into revelation through our practised agent provocateur carry-on.

'What did you think of *Neighbours* last night?' Best to begin in a non-committal, open-ended sort of way. Sylvie was my target, a smiley, generous girl in my class.

'I *know*. Poor Charlene.' This was *Neighbours* hey-day: Charlene and Scott, Harold and Madge, Jim and his ruthless son.

The trick was to keep Sylvie talking, with encouraging but

vague noises of agreement, moving her, once enough info had been unearthed about *Neighbours*, on to *Top of the Pops* or *Jim'll Fix It.* All going well, by the time the bus reached school, I would be sufficiently armed for the day ahead, ready to start my very own Last Night's TV conversations: 'Did you see what Scott did to poor Charlene? He's so *mean*.'

What was the alternative? Admit that we weren't allowed to watch anything? No, thanks, we were perfectly weird enough already.

Even now, I have a passing acquaintance with the plot lines of soaps and dramas I've never seen. Scott and Charlene inhabit some part of my psychological hinterland too, even though I doubt I could pick them out of a police line-up.

'But Everyone Else Does...'

The argument 'but everyone else does', rather than having a softening effect on my mother's resolve, was like a red rag to a bull. Proof, if she had needed it, that she was on the right track.

These ideas about TV rotting the brain were very much her own. Then she read *The Closing of the American Mind*, and all was finally lost.

Alan Bloom was a fifty-something American academic when he wrote a book about the failures of the university system. He was mainly complaining about liberal relativism and how it was destroying moral imperatives. But he had a couple of chapters on 'rock music' and especially Mick Jagger, who he had a real bee in his bonnet about. Basically, his point about rock music is that it's fake, all mouth and no trousers. That it hypes up an idea of sexuality that's sterile and purely commercial, pretending to embrace the spirit of rebellion inherent in teenagers, but really just luring them in and selling them back to the money managers; the ultimate double-cross, as seen in every heist movie ever made, from Hitchcock to Bond.

It's hardly very new now, but at the time, this was like an electric shock to my mother, with her then three teenage children, and three more coming up behind.

She had known there was something not right about the whole scene, instinctively found herself repulsed by the idea of kids acting out their internal craving for excitement and drama via the carefully packaged offerings of the pop world. But now Bloom had really crystallised her thinking and armed her against it, and us. This was not going to be easy, but my mother has always scorned 'easy' where 'right' is involved.

For us, the blow could not have come at a worse time. Somehow, a minute process of normalisation had begun to creep into our hilarious and exciting but definitely odd family life. Somehow, some small relaxations had occurred. I was allowed to go to discos – I think because my parents thought I looked 'sweet' in my red rara skirt and obviously had no idea of the amount of snogging that went on at them. *The Breakfast Club* had crept in under the radar, sometimes even *Dynasty* if my parents were out on a Friday night.

Love Blonde

I had a few records and a crappy portable record player that the large Flemish lady across the road had given to me. I owned Captain Sensible's 'Wot' (you've got to start somewhere), 'Moonlight Shadow' by Mike Oldfield and Maggie Reilly – how I longed for a billowing white cloak and a dead boyfriend who I could mourn forever – and 'Love Blonde' by Kim Wilde. Goodness knows why I didn't have 'Kids in America', a much better song, but maybe that, too, is the story of my life.

Obviously I wasn't allowed to play these records anywhere my parents could hear them. The idea of a daughter who played records was still a sensitive one, and the sound of that whiny 80s guitar grated on their nerves just as much as it now grates on my husband's, but in the confines of my room, I could put on these three records over and over again and try to work out what my eventual moves would be when I was ready to go public with them. I still shared a room with Bridget, but we were now located in the basement because although it was dark and rather forlorn, it felt like the right kind of place to be. Far away from everyone. Sort of nihilistic.

Kim was everything I wanted to be. Blonde, incredibly pouty, with a tight black leather dress and lots of guys staring at her, proof of her wanton desirability.

My mother hated Kim Wilde anyway, because she was 'knowing' and had the kind of dead-eyed coy sexuality my mother despised. (This was the 80s. *Everyone* had a dead-eyed coy sexuality, or tried to.) But then she read Alan Bloom, and suddenly Kim wasn't just an annoying pop-puppet. She was everything that was wrong with a scene my mother instinctively despised, and a daughter she had begun to find baffling.

Now, given that my mother wanted to annihilate Kim, she could have got her on not being able to dance for toffee – a kind of swooping two-step; very lame – but she got so incensed that she took her eyes off the prize and went in with a sledgehammer where a bit of subtle mockery might have been more effective.

It was the lines 'Eyes'll flash and lips will smile/And she'll just tease them for a while' that really got her. My mother has always been dead against teasing. So having got the notion that Kim was glorifying a transactional kind of sexuality, she acted decisively.

I came home from school one day and began the usual business of finding something to eat that didn't contain wheat germ or require twenty-four hours to cook properly, when my travels took me to the bin.

There, in the bin, was Something. A record. 'Love Blonde'. Bent, viciously scratched, covered with green washing-up liquid.

Tweedledum catching sight of his broken brand new rattle could not have been more incensed. I quivered with rage. In those days I often quivered with rage, such was my insatiable appetite for drama, even before I had worked out what to be angry about.

'*Emily...*' Michael, my kind and temperate older brother, the only person who could reliably restrain me, sounded a warning note. But I was well beyond warnings. The damage was so ... pointed. So premeditated. A clean break of the record could have looked like a moment of madness. This was quite clearly the product of hard work. Malice aforethought.

'*Arrrggghhhhhhh!* I howled, a primal cry of pain, hands clutching for something to rend. 'I will *never* forgive her!'

I should point out that even in the throes of insisting I would never forgive her, I could actually also see the funny side of it. Except that obviously I kept that well hidden. Fourteen And Furious was not the moment for nuanced psychological responses. Not when I had been handed Justified All Out Fury on a plate. Even now, the idea of my mother deciding to take her dislike of Kim Wilde to the max, and wrestling with this record, makes me laugh.

She later confessed to Michael that she had tried to simply break it, but it's harder to break 45 inches of black vinyl than you might think. Hence the savage bending, followed by scratching, to put it well beyond use. I'm not quite sure about the washing-up liquid – possibly just a final flourish of hatred for Kim.

The record was replaced – fair was fair, even for my mother – with something innocuous and 'novel', maybe by 'Weird Al' Yankovic. And my obsession with Kim Wilde lasted until Madonna came along and showed me that you could add a little bit of wit and cleverness to the dead-eyed sexuality, and the effect would be much better.

Even now, I will always go as Madonna to any fancy dress party.

Normally I veer towards 'Papa Don't Preach' (the stripy top, not the corset and cropped leggings) or 'Vogue'. Bridget always, always works the 'Like a Virgin' look, and totally trumps me.

I think the worst of it is that I couldn't even dismiss my mother as frumpy and out of touch. She was dazzling, and having a very fun time. For the first time since 1970, when my brother Michael was born, she actually had a bit of freedom. Yes, she had a small baby – Baba – but she also had teenage daughters who, when not sulking and yearning (me) or obsessively cataloguing photos (Bridget), were more than happy to mind Baba. We loved Baba. He was the sweetest, easiest baby ever, and from the day he came home from hospital he was a reliable source of delight in my life, which just then mostly veered between wallowing in despair and crushing boredom.

My mother was in the heyday of her forties when I was at my podgiest teenage worst. She was getting dressed up, going to parties, giving parties and having a gay and glamorous time, while I was counting spots and split ends, waiting for Life to come and find me.

This is one very, very good argument for older mothers. When my daughter is a teenager, I will be an old has-been fifty-something. The stage will be left decently clear for her. She will own the field, as she will undoubtedly feel she should.

Forever Out of Step

'But it made you so enterprising!' said a friend of mine, Clare, who doesn't allow her sons to watch TV when I tried to plead their case on the basis of knowing what they were going through. Her son had been jeered at in Montessori because he suggested a game based on *SpongeBob* – the only kids' TV show he's ever seen – when *everyone* knows that it's all about *Ben 10* these days. He was upset. So was she when he told her, but still adamant. No TV.

'He will be forever out of step,' I tried to explain. 'He will spend the rest of his life wondering what people mean when they say things like "when they met, it was *moy-dah*!" and all laugh together. He will lack cultural references and the common touch. He will feel like he was raised in a parallel universe, and for years he will be on the back foot when his peers discuss the only thing open to them – TV. He will feel *odd*.'

What I didn't say, but thought, was, 'He already doesn't like football. You're not giving the kid a sporting chance here.'

None of my arguments washed with Clare, even when I explained to her that my 'enterprise' that she so admires is entirely confined to the business of finding out stuff about programmes I've never seen, that it stops dead there and doesn't translate into any other aspect of my life. She's not having it. 'You turned out fine,' she insists. And so I cannot help her poor little boys. They must make their own path on this, just as my siblings and I had to. Except Baba. By the time he was old enough to care about TV, my mother had relaxed so completely that she let him watch what he liked. Sometimes I think he was actually raised by a different mother than the rest of us.

Clare's belief is that by denying her kids TV, she will open the door to books. If they don't watch, they will read. Like my mother, she too thinks TV will rot their brains. She might be right, but I have found it very hard to get worked up about this.

Left alone, I probably wouldn't much bother with TV, but that would be out of sheer indifference and thrift rather than any strong feelings about the evils it brings. However, I'm married to a man who watched TV every day of his life as a child, anything he wanted, and who can't see a thing wrong with it. He has made it perfectly clear that if it comes to a choice – me or the TV – he's sticking with the TV, and my two older children have agreed.

'If the TV goes, we go,' they have all cheerfully intoned. No ambiguity there.

Once I realised that I had to make up my own rules on this one, like an adult, rather than just drift along, I had a little think and discovered that far from finding something appalling in TV's appeal, I think it's brilliant and a godsend. I'll never forget the sheer joy of the day when my daughter, then two, sat silently in front of *Peppa Pig* for fifteen minutes and angrily shrieked 'want piggy!' when it was over.

'Reliable peace at last,' I thought. 'Silence on tap. Of course, I must treat it with the care afforded to bomb disposal, lest it blow up in all our faces and create a moronic monster (see, the old teachings die hard), but eternal vigilance has always been the price of peace. And in this instance, a small one to pay.'

TV is a friend and helper. Better than an au pair at the end of a long day (you don't have to feed it or listen to it pining for Bavaria, and your children will never say 'she's not as nice as the last one' about it).

It is also, in my life, proof that we are more than the sum of our experiences. That a habit of independent thought can be achieved. That I can, when I need to, find my own path through this maze of childrearing rather than just parroting the things my mother did.

However, I have drawn the line at things like Wii and Xbox. They clearly, *clearly* rot the brain. They probably make people wheeze too.

PART III
AFTER BIRTH

Chapter 14

THE MOTHER OF ALL MADNESS

*In which I discover that motherhood is a question of
'types', just like being a Spice Girl*

Catherine and I had our first babies at about the same time:
a girl for her, a boy for me. We discovered that we had far
more in common than we had previously thought, this
having always been a distant sort of friendship.

'We must respond to their every cry,' we agreed. 'Only then
can they start to trust the world and their ability to make an impact
on it.'

'Co-sleeping is so much better. It's the most *natural* way.'

We walked round parks together, wearing our babies in slings so
they could feel close to us at all times, decaf soya lattes in hand
(lactose is *so* difficult for babies to digest), stopping to feed on
demand as often as required, in perfect harmony with our vision of
the duties owed to small babies.

Then one day Catherine said, 'I've been trying sleep training on
Bonnie. It's actually working.'

Sleep training? The term we had agreed was actually a soft-soap euphemism for vicious neglect?

'You mean leaving her to cry?' Judgement bristled in every word I uttered.

'She only cried for twenty minutes the first night, and now she's sleeping through.'

'*Twenty minutes!*' I said, closely followed by a silent, wistful aside, 'Sleeping through?', before I righted myself and reattached to my sworn principles.

Fire! Famine! Betrayal! Had we not agreed about the psychological damage (undoubtedly) caused to a child whose every whimper was not greeted with a flurry of soothing activity? How it (surely) created a breach between mother and baby that could never be healed? And there she was, telling me 'she only cried for twenty minutes the first night'.

She might as well have said, 'I started the dismembering by removing her arms and legs...'

Ten years later, I care far less about the minutiae of how women bring up their children. It's no longer a deal-breaker to find them locked into prescriptive routines or floating so free that the child doesn't even have a bed, let alone a bedtime. But I am amazed to find that the rest of society seems to have gone the other way, and is now positively addicted to cataloguing mothers according to type.

So which one are you? Umbrella Mother? Helicopter Mother? Hugger Mother? Tiger Mother? Eagle Mother? Tortoise Mother? Frightened Mouse Mother? Actually, I made those last ones up, but I bet you wouldn't have guessed, because in this era of Mommy Madness, they are perfectly plausible.

The question is, who started the Mommy Wars? And when did they go nuclear?

French or Asian? It's Not a Take-away

There are now as many ways to parent as variations of the flu virus or styles of kitchen. Every six months a new 'type' is identified and written about, whereupon all the rest of us rush to examine this brave new creation to see how she measures up to us and what we're doing. Is she better than us (heaven forbid)? Or by looking at her *modus operandi*, can we feel smug about ourselves in comparison (a much better outcome)? Sometimes we examine her dark arts in order to improve – perhaps Eskimo mothers really do have something to teach us Westerners about *Keeping Babies Warm* – but mostly we do it through curiosity and the desire for comparisons that flatter ourselves.

When it was all about the Tiger Mother, that ferocious Chinese creation who withholds praise and expects straight-A over-achievement from her kids, we could comfort ourselves with the thought that if our children were going to end up less successful than hers, at least they would be happier.

Then, when we got bored with the Asians, enter a wave of books telling us how great French kids are because they eat everything and don't talk back. That was easily dealt with. They might eat asparagus coated in sheep brains and even ask for seconds, but anyone who has spent time chatting to little French kids will know that they are also ferociously judgemental and lacking in solidarity with other children. They are brought up to be mini adults, are dressed as mini adults (often, for some reason, like little English gentlemen off on a sporting weekend; duck shooting, perhaps) and so they behave like mini adults. Divided from each other, and conquered, they respond by telling tales and finding anything unfamiliar (except food; they love unfamiliar food, remember) a cause for suspicion and hostility.

I should know – I was brought up among kids like these. Little bourgeois Belgian children have identical upbringings to French children. They would behave with extreme politeness as long as adults were present – kissing everyone on each cheek, responding '*oui, madame*', '*non, madame*' and standing quietly until spoken to. Then, once the adults had withdrawn, they would stick their tongues out at us, jeer at our less-than-perfect accents and give us a long list of Things That One Must Not Do, such as putting shoes on the sofa, taking two biscuits, talking loudly and playing with the piano unless Maman was there.

Not bringing my children up in the French model is one of the easiest decisions I ever had to make. I would far rather have an unruly brood of noisy, even impolite children who are fundamentally kind and have had the freedom to pursue their own interests, even if these are as inane as flushing things down toilets and bashing Batman figures together, than the well-mannered, stilted, unimaginative French and Belgian children of my childhood acquaintance.

But back to the army of Types that motherhood has somehow spawned. 'What kind of mother are you going to be?' is the unspoken question in Society's eyes as soon as you have a baby. 'Um, a good one, I hope.' Not a proper answer!

You see, it's like picking teams. You have to show allegiance to one or another method of childrearing, and each method comes with its own set of banners and colours, by which I mean the importance placed on specific aspects of the child's development. With the Asians, it is of course achievement; for the French, it's food and manners; for the English, it's being brave and being a good sport. Attachment Parents are all about security and love. Routiners aim for just that – routine; everything in its place and time. The Higher Consciousness ones aim for infant enlightenment, and the many in between pick sides and are told to stick to them with the consistency that is the Number One Rule of parenting. I am dead against consistency, by the way. In a thoroughly inconsistent world, it seems to me we are just setting our kids up for a fall if we persist in being utterly consistent at all times.

The thing is, we're not Spice Girls. Why should we be forced into one or another 'system' and given a bright little label? Sporty Mum, Scary Mum (bags that one!), Baby Mum (hmmm), Posh Mum and, um, Ginger Mum…

The real problem is that so many of these 'types' are mutually antagonistic. The mother who believes in routine and letting them cry it out is appalled by the self-indulgence of the mother who lets Baby sleep in her bed and feeds on demand every time the child opens its mouth to squawk. Ditto the mother who is baby-led in all things and believes the cry-it-out mother is damaging her child psychologically by not responding to its needs.

I'm making light of this, but the antagonism can be very real, driven as it is by a small inner voice that repeats 'my way is best' and that is so invested in believing this assertion to be literally, demonstrably true that it feels the need to knock everything alien in its path.

Tribal Warfare

Not one of us is prepared to entertain the notion that we are bringing our children up badly. Of course we're not. That would be like buying our kids T-shirts saying 'I'm With (Mean and) Stupid' and an arrow pointing straight to us.

We need to believe that whatever system we have in place, even when it barely deserves to be dignified with that term, is a good one that will result in happy, healthy, successful children. And so whatever differs widely from our way must automatically be 'the wrong way'. And because 'our way' is, we like to think, the product of deep exploration into and understanding of the complex psychology of a child, anything that goes against it is obviously not just 'wrong' in the way that five is the wrong answer to 'what's two plus two', but doing terrible damage to boot.

There may always have been an element of this, but ever since Society has provided us with so many convenient labels, the Art Of Mommy War has become much easier and more open. No more nebulous, hidden enemies, just banner-waving partisans with their colours nailed firmly to their masts. This is the moment where Society, not content with brow-beating us from above, encourages us to turn on each other and fight it out in the arena of childrearing, having first equipped us with shield and tridents in the form of self-belief and a tribe.

Because it's easier to do this if you feel like you're part of a gang, that at your back (metaphorically, not literally) are other mothers with the same belief system as you, all ready to do battle (again, metaphorically – I'm not expecting an army of Hugger Mothers all ready to wrap their arms round their opponents and bear-hug them to death). The kind of negative definition we're all guilty of – 'I'm a Baby-Led Mother, not one of those mean Routine Queens who deny their child affection except at scheduled times' – only ramps up the antagonism, as does the kind of slightly hysterical language used in so many baby books.

In order to justify itself and its system, whatever book you've chosen to be guided by in pursuing your course of motherhood needs to annihilate the opposition by painting lurid, awful pictures of what becomes of children who are brought up that way (not by name, of course, but it's pretty easy to identify the targets). In so doing, it naturally leaves you wondering how on earth Sharon-from-playgroup can possibly justify her adherence to Baby Whispering. Doesn't she realise little Jess is going to become a needy, dependent, insecure adult because of it?

We invest an awful lot of ourselves in these labels, and we form bonds and friendships based on them. Which, as I found out, can fall apart when someone goes off-message.

The Wisdom of Foresight

Before actually having children, we all know exactly the kind of mother we're going to be. It's easy – we're going to be carbon copies of dear old Mary Poppins, of course. Mary Poppins Mum is kind, patient and calm. She always has something delicious and wholesome baking in the oven and is a whizz at imaginative games with paper and pencil. Mary Poppins Mum organises jolly playdates and whips the other local mothers into regular fun-but-educational outings. She is never without wipes and plasters in case of emergency and even does finger painting, though her house manages to remain immaculately clean and tidy. Firm but fair, she is the Barbara Woodhouse of childrearing, a Domestic Goddess with a Montessori diploma.

Sadly, for most of us the first child no sooner arrives than Mary Poppins Mum metaphorically gathers up her carefully puréed organic carrots, hand-painted mobiles and Beatrix Potter books and vanishes into the ether, to emerge only very sporadically ever after. There is something about the realities of small children that is wholly incompatible with that particular seductive fantasy. If you ask me, it's no accident that Mary Poppins was a nanny, not a mother.

In her absence, we are left floundering, trying to formulate some kind of coherent approach to what is a messy, inconsistent business. Most of us quickly realise that deep inside, hand in hand with the adorable wraith that was Mary Poppins Mum, lurks something I call Screaming Supermarket Mum. We all know her – she's the one dragging a yelling two-year-old along the sweets-and-chocolate aisle, pausing to hiss, 'Just you wait until I get you home' through gritted teeth.

At this stage, either you pledge allegiance to a system or you are on your own. And sometimes – times like these, when you have a bewildering amount of newness in your life and are feeling pretty lonely anyway – being on your own is not what you want. There is comfort, and safety, in numbers. And so we pick a system and stick to it as best we can.

Frankly, most of us are quite simply Random Mums. Patient one day, ratty the next; sometimes calm and gentle, often irritable and snappish; endlessly aspiring to reason and enlightenment, while generally making snap decisions based on the circumstances of the moment. We are no particular type, just a collection of our good luck and bad mistakes.

But even then, we feel the need to construct a coherent identity out of the miscellaneous scraps of motherhood, a thread through the labyrinth that we can follow to a desirable conclusion. Because what's at stake here is the ultimate prize – who can bring up the 'best' child. Even those of us who protest that 'all we want is for them to be *happy*' do so in the belief that 'happy' equals 'best'.

Glittering Prize

Everyone's version of 'best' varies. For some, it's simple and achievement based: straight As, mastery of modern languages, captain of the first rugby team. For others, it's more nebulous: being a 'good' person, filled with kindness and intuition. Our children's happiness is a key goal for all of us, but definitions of happiness vary so widely. And of course, a little (or a lot) of our own hang-ups and insecurities come into the mix each time.

If you were deeply unassertive as a child and felt this resulted in you being pushed around a bit, there's an excellent chance that you will encourage your own child to stand up for themselves, even if it means they risk going overboard the other way and becoming some kind of karate-chop-first-ask-questions-later maniac. If your life was made troublesome by a fear of water, you're likely to make sure this doesn't repeat itself by getting your child swimming lessons almost before they can walk. And if on the off chance you think you're perfect, then of course you will encourage your child in all the wonderful aspects in which they resemble you.

None of us are immune to reading considerable amounts of back story into our children's behaviour and attributes. This is mostly harmless, even beneficial. Instead of being deeply frustrating, the carry-on of a child who doesn't listen and is constantly lost in his or her own fantasy world can be shrugged off, even admired: 'Oh, he's so like Uncle Jack, always daydreaming.' Assuming that you *like* Uncle Jack, that is. If you don't like Uncle Jack, or if daydreaming is a characteristic of your own that you think has stopped you from knocking the socks off life in the way you would have hoped, then you're not going to take kindly to it in your child.

Essentially, your efforts to ensure your child's happiness, though well meaning, are murky. Because you are You, the product of all your many, various experiences, and you cannot leave yourself and your own complex psychology out of the equation when you try to ensure your child's happiness. Your efforts are contaminated. Which is fine, just as long as we're aware of this simple fact.

There is a disingenuous expression that tries to cover aspiration up, disguise it – it's the notion of encouraging a child to 'be the very best that they can be'. See what the phrase does? It carries a little *moue* of disarmament, throws up its arms in denial and does a distancing sort of shimmy. 'These are not *my* thwarted ambitions being played out,' the phrase implies. 'Oh *no*. All I'm doing is helping this child reach their full potential, whatever that might be, and if it's to be a bus driver, then so be it.' Which is never true. Parents intent on helping their child 'to be the very best that they can be' always envisage head of NASA, CEO of a publicly quoted company or violin prodigy as their child's very best – never bin man or lowly admin assistant.

In the Mommy Wars, extra points are given for this kind of dissembling, because the trick is to pretend that all this has nothing to do with *your* ambitions and desires – it's all about the kids. And unless you are actually a Stage School Mum, burning with thwarted ambition as you push little Billy or Tracy into tap, ballet and modern dance, then it's really quite easy to keep your hand hidden.

But you know what? I'm ready to let go.

Ten years into this business of childrearing, I understand one simple, fundamental thing: every one of us loves our children and wants to do our best by them. Within the context of our lives, we come up with a workable formula, which we constantly adapt and tweak according to changing demands. Even more simply put, we do our best.

I know mothers who work full time, part time and not at all (outside the home, that is). I know mothers who breast-fed, some who didn't, some who breast-fed one child and not another. I know mothers who merrily feed their kids oven chips and sugary yoghurts and those who will not willingly allow a morsel of processed food past their little darlings' lips. I know mothers who let their babies cry it out and others who are baby led in everything from sleeping to potty training.

I do not know a single mother who doesn't hope she's doing her best for her children, given her particular circumstances. I don't know a single mother who doesn't adore her children, who wouldn't do anything in her power for those kids. She may be misguided (although that's not for me to say) and there's a good chance she's simply doing whatever works at any one time without any particular course of action plotted out, but there is no doubt about her motives.

We might not like their hair, or their choice of buggy, or the way they talk to their children (saying 'Well *done*, Maisie, that's a hexagon. Hexagon, Maisie' to a six-month-old is likely to raise hackles in all but the most forbearing of us). We may think their chosen 'system' of childrearing is bonkers, but let's give credit where it's due.

Philip Larkin was undoubtedly right when he said 'They fuck you up, your mum and dad', but I truly believe those parents were actually trying to 'tuck you up'. They just got it a bit wrong.

I Did It My Way

I did eventually try sleep training on my eldest, by the way. I did exactly what the books said: I put him in his cot, awake, having performed a little bedtime routine, kissed him and said good night. He was about eight months old, and I don't think he had ever fallen asleep anywhere except in my arms. There was silence. I tiptoed downstairs, heart hammering, thinking, 'Wow, maybe this stuff does work after all...'

Then, heartbroken wails rising to a crescendo. A fever pitch of despair and abandonment. I sat on the bottom stair, biting my nails and then crying while he howled upstairs, unrelenting, inconsolable, all his worst fears about this world he had been born into finally confirmed. I could see that in a funny way he had just been waiting for this moment, proof that we were inadequate, hopeless parents, not to be trusted. The wailing continued, my crying continued. Eventually, after ten or fifteen minutes, I broke. He clearly wasn't going to. I ran back upstairs, hysterically yelling, 'I'm coming, Baby, I'm coming.' My tone of voice was probably further proof that something appalling had just been done to him. He redoubled his cries, sobbing breathlessly. I scooped him up, spilling tears and apologies. And I never tried crying-it-out on a child again. My nerve was well and truly broken.

'Know thyself,' I thought sadly but sternly. 'Only attempt what you are capable of.'

I do not, for what it's worth, think sleep training is inherently a bad thing. I have friends who accomplish it without fuss or fear, smoothly manoeuvring their babies into excellent sleep patterns that allow the entire house to get unbroken nights. They do this without themselves descending into the horrors and believing they have psychologically scarred their children for life. I have an admirable Dutch friend who believes it's good for the children to learn that not everything can happen Now! just because they want it to. For her, it's a life lesson, not just an unbroken night. And her kids are adorable, not scarred at all.

But I am not Dutch, and there is no point in me doing things that make me hysterical and unhappy. Because that *will* have a psychological impact, on me at least. I may well find myself looking at my grown-up child twenty years from now and thinking, 'He didn't get a First and it's because I didn't pick him up when he cried at night; it's all my fault.' And that is a piece of absurdity to be avoided at all costs.

If something is going to cause you guilt and misery, don't do it. Even if the baby books say you *should.*

Know thyself, then do it your way.

Chapter 15

SCHOOL GATE STYLE

In which I refuse to have a Brazilian

Shortly before I got pregnant for the first time, pants suddenly got very, very small and jeans became very low waisted. Before my life had anything to do with babies, this was quite a good look. Low-slung jeans clinging to hips, a top that nearly met the jeans, leaving just a quarter of an inch of taut(ish) midriff visible when one stretched or twisted. It wasn't the Dawn Of The Mini as fashion moments go, but it was quite nice. Sort of sexy, in a casual, post-grungy, early 2000s kind of way.

Sadly, that was one fashion equation that simply did not have room for a baby. Obviously, the quarter inch of midriff had to be put away immediately, on the basis that it was now several inches, arranged in the wrong direction. The low-rise jeans, even quite apart from the squeezing-back-into-them aspect, were an unmitigated disaster. Bearable when you were standing, they became tricky once you sat down and impossible if Life required you to hunker down or bend over. And Life with small children will always require you to do that.

Picture this: I'm strolling along a busy street, small child in tow, buggy, a couple of shopping bags. Small child decides to get cross about something and is busy shouting at me, using a series of sounds I don't understand with increasing urgency. I bend to his level, like all the good books say you should, and put on my best 'calm mummy' voice.

The effect is marred substantially by the expanse of builder's bum, vast as Ben Nevis, visible to anyone behind me, and even more so by my acute consciousness of this exposure. I'm doing an agonised shimmy – tugging top down and jeans up, wondering which knickers I'm wearing today and how much of them is on display, all while trying to diffuse the impending meltdown. People are sniggering and builders are whooping, and who could blame them? One rather beautifully groomed older lady burst right out laughing. 'Best days of our lives,' she said firmly to me as she passed. Women like her make the world a better place.

The Politics of Grooming

In the good old days, when nearly all new mothers looked a bit wild and unkempt, it didn't matter. Now that so few do, it does. Suddenly, *not being groomed* has become a political statement – as if by failing to get your hair done and wear a simple yet charming outfit, you're saying, 'Look at me! I eat whole foods and believe in extreme breast-feeding' rather than demonstrating a simple, practical response to having very little time and very few clothes that fit properly.

By not keeping up with the accepted image of motherhood, we are seen to be signalling something far more than just 'I'm too busy to find another clean top, and anyway Baby is only going to smear it again'.

There is nothing at all wrong with eating whole foods (I wish I did more of it) or extreme breast-feeding, but it's wrong that this presumption should be made about those of us who have simply opted to wear the first thing that came to hand and put our hair into a scraggy ponytail.

If we aren't making an effort, it's because we couldn't be bothered to make an effort. Or because on the scale of the many other things we have to do, including wrestling a struggling infant into a buggy and checking the nappy bag, all while racing against the clock of the next feed, Making An Effort just didn't make the grade. *Not* because there is some deeper, underlying significance to our lack of effort.

The Kaftan Conundrum

Whatever about looking passable when pregnant, trying to make the grade once the baby is born is when the real challenge begins. Living up to all this Yummy Mummy stuff when you no longer have time to get dressed in the mornings or before going out, no time to consider which outfit works best and how to accessorise properly, is a whole different kind of tedious.

If you're breast-feeding, there is also the question of finding clothes that will allow you to do it at a moment's notice without exposing your entire, enormous stomach to whatever roomful of people you happen to be in. So you need a top that pulls down, not up, thereby automatically discounting every dress you own. But you don't want it to pull down too far, because that would expose too much boob to the roomful of people. The top can't be tight, either, or it won't pull anywhere, up or down. It will stick halfway, with bits of you bulging on either side. Not the look any of us are hoping for.

As if breast-feeding in public wasn't generally an occasion for self-consciousness anyway (even when people are *not* staring, they are so carefully not staring that really, they might as well just stare) without adding absurd, inappropriate clothes into the mix. Such is the transformative power of fashion that the 'wrong' versus 'right' top can make the experience bearable – i.e. you are decent, comfortable, discreet – or utterly shaming. I'm not a particularly shallow person – most of me doesn't give a damn what I look like at such moments or what the people, so carefully not staring, think. But a small bit of me does, I confess it.

Now how many tops that tick all these boxes do any of us own? Of course they can be bought, usually from dedicated websites, but that's expensive, and while you might invest in one or two, you're unlikely to buy many more than that. And yet you may well be breast-feeding many times a day for several months. One or two tops aren't going to go far.

This is why I've been caught out, more often than I can bring myself to remember, trying hastily to arrange coats, bags, even a newspaper over whatever fleshy roll is being exposed in cafés, at other people's houses, on park benches. Baby yells, you have no choice but to feed him or her. They don't care that in so doing you will have to reveal your still-flabby stomach to the passing world. And so I would sit, teeth gritted against the embarrassment, knowing that no matter how skilfully I rearranged the jacket or newspaper, there was still a roll of flesh protruding at some inappropriate point. Depending on how much exposure was going on, I could sometimes feel the chill wind of social disapproval right along with the chill wind of the wind.

If you aren't breast-feeding, this is one piece of sartorial misery you have spared yourself. However, you still have the problem that anything nice in your wardrobe doesn't fit, and anything that does fit isn't nice. I call it the Kaftan Conundrum – if we can actually wear it, it looks hideous – and it's responsible for the badly harmonised collection of velour bottoms and outsized T-shirts that so many of us resort to post-baby.

I'm convinced there is also an element of subconscious but

wilful invisibility to the velour bottoms and outsized T-shirts. It's a way of signalling to Society – given that Society has evolved to no longer allow us a period of natural invisibility – that we do not wish to be noticed just yet, thank you. That we are not ready to resume our places amongst the ranks of those 'in the game', and that when we are, we will signal this by donning a tailored blazer and a new pair of jeans.

On top of not fitting into any of your clothes properly anymore (just because you can close the zip doesn't mean it *fits*), you have missed at least one, if not two, 'seasons' – which is about 100 years in the fashion world. Naturally, we all snigger a little at the word 'season' and the suggestion that any of us would actually go out shopping with the purpose of 'updating our wardrobes' in mind. But if you think about it, we probably buy a couple of things every couple of months, and these things somehow keep our wardrobes ticking over so that even though, obviously, we never have anything to wear, we don't actually have *nothing* to wear, either.

Missing those little bits of buying – a new jacket here, a couple of cute T-shirts there, maybe a pencil skirt if we're feeling exciting – will have far more impact than you might expect. Once you are 'back in the game' of wanting to get dressed in a coherent sort of way, you will, if you are anything like me, find that your wardrobe seems to have been stripped back in the months since you last looked at it, like a pine table about to be varnished. That is, plain and barely functional.

And unless you're the sort of person who heads off to boutiques, credit card in hand, and a list of required items – 'One top, black, low cut. One cardigan, cashmere, long...' – or who browses the Boden catalogue and actually places orders rather than just musing, then it will take you a good year to make up for those 'missing seasons'.

Brazilian? Is that a Nut?

Mostly, though, we buy into the notion of the Yummy Mummy and do our best to recreate it, offering it up to Society as a token of our good faith around this whole 'mother' business. A kind of visual code for the hearty, reassuring message, 'Don't worry, we're not going to go off-side on this one and start making yoghurt out of our own breast milk; we'll keep our end up.'

And so we take on the extra time burden and the extra expense of trying to have appropriate clothes and a decent standard of grooming. I take a lot of shortcuts, but I do keep things faintly ticking over. My rule of thumb here is, if I suddenly got invited to the Oscars followed by a pool party in the Chateau Marmont, could I be ready in six hours? Or if my husband decided to sell me for a million euro to Robert Redford, would Redford demand his money back in shock at the sight of a body that has spent too long under dust wraps?

It's not that I think either of these things are very likely (on balance, I'm thinking the Oscar–Chateau Marmont invite is a fraction more to be expected, but that's just me; you might be the sort to attract elderly millionaires with ease), just that if they did happen, could I say yes or would I have to mutter something about it not being a good time, and maybe later? If I couldn't say yes because I knew that the process of making myself look presentable was a six-day event rather than six hours, involving a deep spring clean rather than a flick with a duster, then I know I need to up the ante on general grooming just a little. I operate a similar system with my house, by the way, only with an expanded timeframe: if Queen Elizabeth suddenly announced her intention of visiting, and of publicly scoring the state of the place out of ten, could I get it ready in six days (quick lick of paint here and there, bit of window washing and maybe, just maybe, some new cushion covers) or would I need six weeks? If six weeks are required, we have slid too far into squalor.

But I do keep it very low key. I wax my own legs (bravo, Boots), do my own nails (when they are not bitten to the quick) and I have a hairdresser who comes to the house every six weeks. That might sound a bit glam, but oh dear, it is not! She cuts and colours my hair and cuts the boys' hair, all for far less than a salon would charge me alone. The entire downstairs gets covered in hair, the boys complain bitterly throughout and I have to get up every couple of minutes throughout my own session to rescue various children from various unpleasant situations of their own making.

In fact, it's all slightly stressful. However, it means I don't have to get a minder just to go to the hairdresser, and I don't have to choke with stress when I see that the salon is running late and I'm not going to be back when I said I was. And I save some money.

I know plenty of women for whom going to the hairdresser is a precious escape, a little bit of time alone that they will never willingly give up, but it just doesn't do it for me. Never has. And so I'm very happy to sacrifice the bit of peace I might get against the dose of stress I might also get.

I've given up on gym memberships and Pilates classes for the same reason – they became just one more source of stress in my life, rather than offering the desired, opposite effect. Having to forfeit the cost of the pre-paid Pilates class because a child has vomited or your minder/partner is stuck in traffic is a little bit like being lightly slapped across the face by an incredibly fit twenty-something wearing yoga pants. It's not conducive to inner peace and outer taut abs, so instead I go for a run whenever I get the chance on the basis that I will never have to text the park to say, 'Sorry! Cant mk it. Cvrd vomit.'

Luckily, I've never been high maintenance. Even in my pre-baby days, I rarely saw the inside of a beauty parlour. The monthly round of facials, eyebrow threading, waxing, massage and general maintenance has never been for me, so the Before-and-After contrast isn't too bad. But I know plenty of women whose standards of presentation are far higher than mine, for whom fitting in the various necessary appointments has become a question of micro-efficient scheduling. They do it because they want to, but also because they feel that they are being judged on these things.

Also, and I consider myself very lucky here, I'm in the cut-off age group for being able to say, 'Brazilian? Isn't that a nut?'

I was pregnant, and therefore had a perfect 'get out of gym' note. Thereafter, I operated on the basis that no one could really expect a mother-of-two-then-three to expose the full extent of the indignities suffered by that area, and that my husband had already seen far more of that particular zone in the delivery room than he ever could have wished. I would honestly be afraid that getting a Brazilian would give him awful flashbacks and he'd start reaching for gas and air or telling me to 'do the breathing!'

I spared the poor man perineal massage when I was pregnant, and I will continue to spare him the gynaecological equivalent of revealing the Third Secret Of Fatima.

The School Run Style Wars

Now, a word about school gates style. Just one word, to start with, but uttered very loudly.

No!

This is one bit of nonsense that has got to stop. I do not care that Claudia Schiffer has perfected the high-waisted 70s jeans look and that it's the perfect school gate look – casual, stylish, practical. I do not care that Gwyneth Paltrow can rock a chunky knit and cowboy boots when dropping Apple to her London school. When I hear of the supposed sartorial judgement that goes on around the picking up and dropping off of kids – the perfect thing to wear, car to drive, scarf to add, bag to carry (oh, but don't try *too* hard, because then you look like a loser – nah nah!) – well, it makes me want to lie down for an hour. This kind of carry-on makes it sound worse than actually *being* at school, and surely that isn't possible?

People, we are better than this. Whatever about all the other stuff – the many millions of things, in this Shouldocracy of ours, that make us feel guilty and inadequate – this is one bit of pressure we need to say no to.

Because it's nonsense. The fantasy of school run style wars is the preserve of celebrity magazines and slow Sundays in September when newspaper editors can't think of anything sufficiently gloomy to run as news. No real person cares about this. I meet women every morning at the school gate, on nights out or at lunch who I know to be madly glamorous and they're wearing fleeces and snow boots. Or a pair of jeans and a jumper. Just normal jeans and a normal jumper, not '70s high-waist jeans' and a 'chunky knit'.

If they're working mothers, they're dressed for work in whatever outfit their work requires, whether it's a nurse's uniform or a charcoal suit. Otherwise they're wearing boring, everyday clothes that bear as much resemblance to 'an outfit' as me painting my house white will make it look like something designed by Syrie Maugham.

I know one woman who does the school run in her pyjamas and slippers. She can't get out of the car, so the sight and sound of her bellowing across the car park to other mothers or her children, telling them to come back for things they have forgotten or reminding them that today is tennis after school, is a familiar one. No one turns a hair.

Chapter 16

MEET MRS MOP

In which I confront motherhood's inner demon

I have an alter ego. Her name is Mrs Mop. Not quite a cleaning lady, nonetheless she is a poor, tired, downtrodden, put-upon specimen of humanity, with a stooped back and weary eyes. Mrs Mop is sullen, passive aggressive and ineffectual. She is not me, and yet, there must be something in me that feels kinship with her. I really have no idea where she comes from – presumably some race memory of motherhood, stretching back into medieval times – but I'm starting to learn when to expect her to appear.

Often, it's when the children won't eat something I've prepared for them (even when I knew damn well they wouldn't eat it because it was bright green or contained wheat germ). Instead of saying 'fine, eat toast' or 'there's nothing else' or whatever my preferred strategy is at such times, I find myself going into a well-worn lament, like the old woman of the roads. 'I've spent all day making that, slaving away here to try and cook you something and all you can do is throw it back in my face. Well, that's the last time I ever...' and so on. And on. The lament is inaccurate to the point of a downright lie, pointless and very out of character.

There is an angrier version of Mrs Mop too. She comes out at the end of a long day when some piece of misbehaviour finally tips the scales. This Mrs Mop goes on a long diatribe: 'I *told* you that would happen if you didn't stop, but oh, no, you wouldn't listen and now I have to tidy *this* up on top of all the other things...' Awful stuff, eh? So why do I do it? I think it's because I can't help it.

What psychological need does Mrs Mop serve? As far as I can work her out, she is the auto pilot in weak moments, a kind of learned response that takes over when I'm annoyed and not energetic enough to assert my own response or ask myself, 'Do I really care that they didn't eat that/broke something? If so, how much do I care and what am I going to do about it that will be constructive?'

When I can't work these things out because I'm tired and ratty anyway, enter Mrs Mop. She is the comforting (because familiar) groove into which my narrative runs. She takes over – droning on and on about how '*typical* of you to *always...*' Mrs Mop doesn't know when to stop, and she's addicted to catastrophe: words like 'always', 'never', 'typical'.

This is because she's an archetype. She is responding to all children, everywhere, who have ever done something naughty or not eaten their dinner. Hers is a memory, bred in the bone, of children with hacking coughs and men down the pub spending the wages. Mrs Mop can't assess an individual situation on its merits or otherwise. All she can do is pick up the ancient mantra of generations of harassed, weary mothers.

My own mother is not at all Irish. She is half Palestinian, half English. She grew up in Africa and never set foot in Ireland until the age of eighteen. Since then, she has lived here for a total of only about ten years, broken into several different chunks. Yet even she is entirely capable of the whole 'oh, don't mind me, I'll just sit here in the dark' thing, which makes me think that the Irish Mother isn't a geographical construct as much as an emotional truth.

I think we all have a version of Mrs Mop – an inner moan who overreacts to quite minor setbacks (Mrs Mop never appears in a crisis; that is not her comfort zone). Mrs Mop isn't good at resolution – she doesn't, for example, instigate time out or whatever other disciplinary system we are using that particular day. She just goes on and on, her discontented hum eventually fading into the background.

My children hate Mrs Mop – not that they have a name for her; they don't need any more ammunition than they already have – and I don't blame them. They also disregard her. They don't listen to the substance of her litany, they just close their ears to the tirade and carry on. My husband hates her too. He has never said so, but I can tell from the set of his shoulders and duck of his head as soon as she gets into full flow. I don't suppose I will ever defeat her entirely, but I like to think of life with children as one long battle against Mrs Mop.

Some of us are better than others at keeping Mrs Mop under control and at arm's length (my own success in this varies greatly and depends on all sorts of things, including what else is going on in other parts of my life) and some of us take a long time to even acknowledge her. But that voice of recrimination is there in all of us. I have known French Mrs Mops, Italian Mrs Mops (the worst kind; they *never* let up), young, old and in-between Mrs Mops.

And I know plenty of women who, having never had a Mrs Mop moment in their lives, are horrified to find her suddenly emerge, fully formed, from their mouths once they have children. 'Where is this stuff coming from?' one friend asked me, appalled, after her first such incident. I couldn't tell her – except that she's in the hinterland of all our psyches in some form – but I could tell her to join the gang.

Chapter 17

In Praise of Women

In which I make the case for a universal sisterhood

'Nice to meet you.' She might have been dropping a dead fly into a wastepaper basket. Efficient but distant.

She was a 'supermodel' (I have to qualify that because she wasn't actually, but that's what the PR people were insisting on). She held out a hand for me to shake, staring glassily at a point behind my shoulder. Taking hold of it was like opening a door onto the Arctic tundra – a blast of icy air whistled past, freezing my eyelashes, fixing my smile rigidly to my face.

'I'm sorry I'm late,' I said. 'The minder was delayed.'

'How old are your children?'

'Five and seven. Boys.'

'Hey' – smile – 'I have a five-year-old too.'

Ten minutes later, we were chatting warmly and amiably, discovering that despite our five-year age difference and the fact that she had legs twice the length of mine and a much better handbag, we actually had loads in common.

Well, we had children, and that's all you need.

Before I had children, I used to wonder what the female equivalent of football talk was – you know, the way men of any age, if they like football, even if they have never met or actively dislike each other, can, if necessary, talk for hours about transfer windows and goal scoring.

Eventually, I gave up. I could find no female equivalent. On being introduced to another woman within an approximate age range, the default setting seemed always to be 'off'.

None of the obvious opening gambits were infallible – job, clothes, make-up, how long it took for a city centre bus to arrive. It seemed that there was a faint note of hostility that characterised the initiation phase of all female interactions, and any one of these topics, no matter how innocently introduced, ran the risk of being considered inflammatory.

Volunteer a remark about your job – even if it was that the new boss seemed to hate you and made you grate Parmesan or staple reports till your fingers bled – and you ran a real risk of being accused of showing off.

Complain that you had waited forty-five minutes in a sub-zero wind for the bus, and instead of sympathy, you might get a smug, 'Oh, I drove in. In my new bright pink VW Beetle. That my boyfriend bought me.'

You would be forgiven for thinking that the kind of girl who would say that could never, ever be a pal. But you'd be wrong. Give her ten years, a couple of kids and a chance to trade in the pink Beetle for something sensible with plenty of boot space, and you may well find a kindred spirit.

Trust Life

The inevitable wearing-away that Life does – of our dreams, our aspirations, our notions of ourselves – is partly responsible for the change. Now please don't think I mean that in a depressing way. I don't. I mean it in a 'hurray for Life!' kind of way. Our dreams and aspirations often bear no resemblance to what we *really* want, because we're young and we have no idea what we really want. We might think we want to be world famous, supernaturally beautiful and mind-blowingly rich. Fast forward ten or fifteen years and those things rarely seem so attractive anymore. We can see the down sides all too clearly and have swapped them for more homely stuff: learn to like myself. Be a good friend. Be happy. Stop obsessing over whether the bathroom needs repainting.

Generally, too, a few years' experience of the random difficulties Life throws in all our paths will have a softening effect on most personalities. The arrogance of youth is very appealing, especially the arrogance of attractive young women, but it does not compare, for quality, with the matured kindness of a grown-up woman who has weathered her share of storms and heartache. Every difficult experience that we survive helps create a more profound and sympathetic character.

Young women believe – as they should believe – that it is all theirs for the taking. That they can aspire to the highest rung, design their life precisely as they want it, have children and carry seamlessly on in their chosen path. They need to believe these things – a huge dash of self-belief is entirely necessary to embark on the scary journey that is Life, especially Life With Kids. If we all read the statistics about what having children does to career paths and earning power and actually believed these stats applied to *us*, we'd never dare. But the arrogance and self-belief of 'that's not going to happen to *me*' is usually mixed with a dash of impatience, a desire to *get on with being fabulous* and not be stuck talking to boring old you.

The veterans amongst us – we who have travelled that route, moving from total belief that having children isn't going to change us *at all* to staring at the unrecognisable shape of our lives some years later and wondering which bits of it we ever formally agreed to – take a slightly guilty pleasure in watching the transformation. It's a clipping of wings in one way, but because we believe it's also an enrichment in others, we don't feel too bad about our enjoyment of the spectacle.

Anyway, Life generally has better plans for us than we have for ourselves. Life is like the kind but firm parent who says 'of course you can't marry him' when we profess undying love for our first boyfriend and insist that we will never look at another. So Life doesn't acquiesce in our teenage dreams of global super-stardom or sleeping with as many rock stars as possible. It gives us other, unexpected paths that are usually far more interesting than we expected.

Partly, too, it is simply that women are, frankly, fantastic; give us enough time and we will prove it. We are, by and large, resourceful, capable, competent and kind. At the age of twenty-two or twenty-three, we are so busy expressing other things – wanton sex goddess, so-sharp-we-cut coolness, busy professionalism – that the rest of it lies dormant, invisible to the naked eye. But once we chill a little on being a sex goddess or boardroom big shot, and as we develop the confidence to just be ourselves, what comes out? Kindness, capability, competency.

And partly it's because kids are the great leveller. You cannot be a precious princess once you have nappies to change and noses to wipe, still less once projectile vomit enters the equation. And you cannot be a jack-booting captain of industry with small children who want to trail around to the shops wearing dirty Supermen outfits and stopping every five paces to stare at a crack in the pavement. In having to adapt these things into our lives – in having to expand our repertoire, as it were – we discover new sides, new depths. And a new kinship with other women.

Other mothers become the only people who really, *really* understand the new dimensions of your life. Your partner (if he is a he) doesn't, no matter how convincing the noises he makes. Your friends without kids most definitely don't (and by the way, you have a serious duty *not* to bore the pants off them by endlessly talking about children).

For an instant dash of ready sympathy and understanding, it is other mothers, every time. I don't mean we're all identical once we have children – far from it; we are still ourselves, after all – and there may be many other areas in which no sympathy exists between us at all (she doesn't care about the environment and drives a huge, gas-guzzling SUV while you walk everywhere and recycle loo paper), but still, you both share a core concern, and that counts for a lot.

The bond between mothers is forged not in the labour ward through common memories of pain, as so often presumed, but in something even more fundamental. It's the experience we all share of having our deepest wish – to be a good and happy mother – daily challenged by the very people we wish to be good and happy mothers to. The heartache and frustration that goes with that is the secret bond between mothers.

The daily failures (of temper, humour, calm, good sense) and daily resolves (to be better) are what unite us, even if these things are rarely acknowledged openly. Still, we know the contents of each other's most secret heart chambers, because they are the same as our own.

How many of us have cried at the challenges of mothering a particular child? Lain awake at night worrying about another child's failure to integrate? Lamented our own inability to stay aloof when confronted by the tantrums of a third? We might not speak of these things – not much, anyway – but we can see them etched into one another's faces, and that knowledge breeds sympathy and tolerance.

These truths are the greatest protection against the demands of Mothershould that you will find. It's like Tinkerbell getting the children to say, 'I believe in fairies!' Every time another mother tells you the truth about her experience – her failures, struggles, efforts, aspirations – you will find greater confidence in your own life.

People in Glass Houses

Anyone with a child is living in a giant glass house, so throwing stones is a stupid thing to do. You can be perfectly certain that if you're foolish enough to boast about your parenting skills, your child will promptly let you down. Tell everyone what a good eater your six-year-old is, and he or she will suddenly refuse anything except white food. Boast that your fourteen-year-old son is such a good boy and never causes you a moment's anxiety, and you can be pretty certain that he'll be picked up by the police for brawling or dealing drugs barely a week later.

This may just be the law of averages, but it seems to me more like the law of smugdom.

You cannot control your children, or even predict them, so you better not expect them to shore up your vision of yourself. That is not their role.

And by the way, there's no time limit on it. You can be made to look retrospectively ridiculous at any stage. Say your child robs a bank when they're fifty-three and you were once rash enough to suggest that you had it all worked out and that the secret of good parenting – said with smug smile – was *patience*, or *quinoa*, or whatever. Well, your friends will all remember the irritation of that remark and will be correspondingly filled with unholy glee at your downfall.

Once we have kids, we're all just one step away from shame and catastrophe. This is why we try hard not to stare at the woman in the supermarket whose child is having a spectacular meltdown because she's not allowed a packet of gummy bears. Her today, us tomorrow.

Older mothers sometimes let the side down on this one. Once their children are grown, they seem to conveniently forget all the tantrums and meltdowns and will tut-tut quietly to themselves when they pass a child shrieking 'I *hate* you! I want those gummy bears!' so hard that her larynx is about to twist.

My own mother can't seem to recall any of us misbehaving, ever, even though I can name-check at least twenty incidents so bad they should have landed us in the hottest water, just off the top of my head.

I have a pink elephant teddy that I'm very fond of that I got when I was about five. When I say 'got', I really mean 'extorted'. I saw it in a shop, asked for it and was told no. I asked again, still no. So I simply picked it up and headed out of the shop, onto the street and kept walking. My parents had to fling money at the shopkeeper and chase after me before I was entirely swallowed up by the crowd. Later that day, having refused to let my little sister play with said elephant, it was taken away and hidden while I was sent to my room.

Any reminder of this episode leaves my mother honestly baffled. In her mind, such things never happened. This is the veil Life draws over itself, the necessary process of forgetting that accompanies everything to do with motherhood.

The Bump Bag

The onset of maternal sympathy begins with pregnancy. Announce that you're expecting, and you'll find that women who have previously viewed you with indifference or suspicion are suddenly *on side* in a concerned and practical way. They will give you advice (often whether you want it or not), suggestions, even their old clothes. All these things are indicators of goodwill, a kind of welcome-to-the-club bonanza.

No matter how badly dressed I was during my first pregnancy – and I was – it would have been much worse if it hadn't been for the Bump Bag. This was a bag of communal maternity wear, passed around in an ever-increasing circle, and it was a lifesaver.

I'm not offering up this information as any kind of self-satisfied 'good housekeeping top tip', like those 'helpful hints' you find on parenting websites: 'I always keep a supply of chopped banana and apple in the freezer for my LD to suck on when his gums are sore…' Bully for you. I award myself Housewife of the Year if I have anything in the freezer at all other than ice and an empty packet of fish fingers.

No, the Bump Bag is more of a metaphor than a boast. At first, this bag contained only the best stuff – clothes we were proud of; the one or two expensive dresses our mothers might have bought for us – and was loaned only to an inner circle of friends. People we could rely on to treat the clothes well, scrupulously following care labels. By the end of my third pregnancy, it contained everything from giant T-shirts to support socks as we worked out, through difficult experience, the sheer volume of clothes required and as our pride was gradually whittled away by necessity. The barriers were down. We mothers and mothers-to-be had stopped pretending to be fabulous to one another and had entered the zone in which we would happily confide to each other about our varicose veins, backache and stress incontinency.

At each new pregnancy, the bag would come back around, with some items that were like old friends and some new exciting stuff. These days, it moves on, out of my sight, like a chain letter of good hope. Possibly one day it will end up on the moon or in the *Guinness World Records*: 'elasticated trousers worn by highest number of pregnant women'.

Later, the same thing happened with baby clothes. At first people are wary of offering them in case one might be offended –

there's a funny thing around second-hand clothes for some – and proffer only the really good stuff, like Petit Bateau and Jacadi. But once I accepted enthusiastically and explained that as kids, my sister and I had mostly been dressed in our cleaning lady's daughter's cast-offs, that was OK and the hand-me-downs came thick and fast – everything from cheap cotton banana-stained babygros to odd mittens.

The Greek Chorus

We women and mothers are each other's greatest supporters and each other's greatest critics. These are two sides of the same coin – the coin being our deep interest in the doings and beings of each others' lives. We are so immersed that it's easy to be supportive, and almost impossible not to be critical. The problem arises when these two things fail to meet constructively. When the criticism is silent or delivered out of earshot, and the support too vociferous.

Because we can be *too* nice. The Greek chorus of 'you go, girl!' can actually drown out the small voice that says 'maybe something *is* amiss' and that could usefully be listened to. The urge to shore up another woman's self-confidence can make us deaf to the reasons behind her insecurity and we can fail to acknowledge that maybe she's *right*, maybe she does need to lose weight/exercise more/stand up for herself.

We are so quick with the soothing comment or compliment that we risk devaluing the whole currency. We tell outright lies sometimes – 'nonsense, you look *great*' – to someone who's complaining of feeling exhausted instead of agreeing that she does look tired but it's nothing a few nights' sleep or a weekend away wouldn't sort out.

We positively fall over ourselves to reassure and flatter. We shore each other up and rush to protect the other's self-esteem, like a SWAT team deployed the instant any woman, anywhere, voices self-doubt or criticism. The mission? Annihilate All Insecurity. Terminate Uncertainty With Extreme Prejudice.

Every time a woman admits to a weakness or insecurity, every other woman in the vicinity will charge in with masking tape and putty to fill in the cracks and stop up the dam. It's like we think one admission of failure will bring the whole structure crashing down around us.

'I'm so hopeless, I'm definitely going to get fired' will inspire 'no, you're wonderful and you're too good for that job anyway', even if 'well, why don't you consider retraining so as to be better at your job, or going for something you like better?' is a more purposeful answer. We never miss an opportunity to make one other feel good, no matter how absurd or unhelpful our denials.

There is, of course, huge strength in this – we all get our very own angel choir to endorse our every decision, to chant us over the finish line, cheering approval at every step. It's very reassuring, a jolly sort of love-bomb, a constant deluge of approval and positive reinforcement.

But – and this is a big old but – the flip side, if you think about it, is that all this positivity is ever so slightly patronising. The endless validation pre-supposes that we women are a feeble lot, with self-esteem so fragile that one harsh word could tip us over into floundering distress. That we can't cope with criticism, no matter how tactfully delivered and well merited.

We women have a genuine role to play in each other's lives. We are the sounding boards for new ideas, the supreme authorities in matters of the heart, the domestic gold standard and recipients of countless confidences. If we could rise to the trust implicit in all that – to tell the truth as we see it, even if it means the initially wounding acceptance that the person in front of us isn't actually perfect, and if that person, instead of crumpling like a heap of used tissues and sobbing 'you're such a *bitch*' could take it on the chin and make some changes – then I think we might sort out many of the ills of the world.

Nowhere is the endless endorsement more apparent than in bringing up children. This is where the Greek chorus really hits its stride, partly due to the not-wanting-to-criticise-because-we're-probably-next-for-a-fall thing, and partly because we understand that support is more valuable than criticism. If women in general activate a SWAT team every time they voice self-doubt, mothers get the full FBI Critical Incident Response Team.

And yet, in no other situation is it more important to tell the truth.

Other women can often see your family situation with a clarity that you don't have because your maternal relationships are just too intense. If you have your nose pressed right up against the tree, how will you ever see the woods? You won't. And so a helpful friend – a genuinely helpful friend, who maybe has kids of her own and definitely has your best interests at heart – can sometimes do the seeing for you.

They have a good vantage point. After all, rows with your children are too often played out in public. Kids, unlike your husband or partner, are not going to wait until you get home and can discuss this reasonably and in private. They are going to go into full battle mode – like Celtic warriors, only without the blue-daubed faces and hair spiked up with lime – wherever they happen to be and everyone is going to be witness to the engagement.

I'm not talking about the odd isolated difference of opinion. I'm talking about the regular low-level problematic interactions. The child who won't stop whinging. Is always teasing her little brother. Constantly fights with other kids. The child who somehow involves you in confrontation on a near-daily basis. The one who causes you sleepless nights as you wonder what has gone wrong (albeit temporarily) in their psyche and how to fix it. The child who causes you to weep with the frustrated desire to make things better, even as you find yourself snapping 'I *told* you before not to do that' at them.

Mostly these matters don't call for serious professional intervention. You don't decide to go see a child psychologist because your seven-year-old is driving you nuts by constantly asking for stuff. And in that case, a well-meaning, trusted neutral party – *not* every random mother at the school gate or in the car-wash queue – can offer a perspective that you entirely lack.

'Perhaps you're being too hard on him.'

'He's frustrated because the baby gets so much of your attention.'

'Have you considered getting her ears tested? I've noticed that she doesn't seem to respond when she can't see your face and I don't think it's stubbornness.'

I'm not being funny here. These are all potentially useful observations. And made by the right person, they can be of tremendous benefit to any mother who's at the end of her tether.

We all owe it to each other not to instantly go into Greek chorus mode every time another mother voices a concern, shouting her down with cries of 'no, you're amazing, it will be fine' before she has even got to the end of her sentence. Instead, let's hear her out, consider what she says carefully and see if there is anything useful we can add to the situation that's troubling her.

After all, as an antidote to the vague aspirational suggestions of the Shoulderati, nothing beats solid, informed assistance. Especially when it's offered in the sure knowledge that the one offering will soon be the one in need, as the tables turn in the never-ending spin cycle that is bringing up children.

Chapter 18

PLAY *WHAT*?

In which I introduce playdates – the office parties of kid land

I knew four was too young for this. What was I thinking, saying yes? I knew it would end in tears, but I hadn't expected highly specific threats of violence.

My eldest son had started Montessori a few months before. It was madly high achieving – the amount of homework that came back every day was far in excess of what the child was getting two years later at the end of senior infants – but he settled, somehow, after some difficult days, and made friends. And that's where the trouble started.

'Why don't you bring him round on Wednesday? The boys can play and we can have a coffee.' Why not indeed?

Her house was geographically close to where we lived, but socially and in real estate terms, it may as well have been the Hollywood Hills. Seven bedrooms for a family of four. Garden the size of a football pitch. A front door that led to a cavernous hallway, where the upper reaches echoed distantly above our heads. Down some giant stairs to an architect-designed, light-filled kitchen about the size of our entire house.

This was playdating right out of our league, the child social equivalent of getting asked out by the coolest boy in your year and knowing, just *knowing*, you were going to shame yourself utterly by choking on your cigarette smoke or sneezing all over the joint and blowing the stuff to the four winds.

I had a vision of the inevitable return visit. I wondered if she would literally be too big for our tiny house. Her feet, used to palatial spaces, might stick out and I would have to leave the back door open to accommodate them. Or she would bump her head on the ceiling when she stood up.

All went well for about half an hour. The mum and I chatted – I silently blessed the instant common ground that establishes itself between mothers. We shared our feelings about the Montessori, about diet, reading, activities and so on. We subtly bitched about some of the teachers and generally had a jolly time. The boys played with Spiderman toys in the playroom. Until:

'I'm going to *kill* you!' Eldest Son had the boy in a headlock and was trying to strangle him. The boy was punching Eldest Son in the sides and back, wherever he could reach.

'Don't worry, it's fine, they're just tired,' the mother gasped. I could see panic in her eyes as ES tightened his grip around the boy's neck.

'Stop it! Leave him alone!' I shouted.

'I won't leave him alone. I'm going to *kill* him. KILL HIM.' He sounded excited, like his purpose in life had just been revealed.

Somehow, we exited. Me half-dragging, half-pushing ES as he made one more valiant effort to *kill* the boy. I was muttering something about how it had been lovely and they must come to us soon, while the other mother still nobly insisted 'they're just tired'.

I learned one thing from that fraught episode. If they are not old enough to go alone to playdates, they aren't old enough to go at all.

It's not that I mind my son threatening to kill other small boys – that seems quite normal to me. But having to sit there and watch him do it is another thing.

In the years since, I have implemented the Playdate Alone Or Not At All rule, which works fine. To a point. It still leaves plenty of scope for nightmare playdates of one sort or another. I have had children who have shouted 'EUGH, THAT'S DISGUSTING' at any food I have put in front of them, even when it was just toast. Who have climbed onto the kitchen counters and looked through all the cupboards, helping themselves to anything they fancied and chucking the stuff they didn't onto the floor. Children who have followed me around all afternoon, telling me things about worms and refusing to play with the child for whose entertainment they were invited. Children who have cried for their mothers barely two minutes in the door. Who have cried when their mothers have arrived to collect them, hanging onto furniture in order not to leave. Children who have whispered 'why didn't you come *earlier*?' to their collecting parent. Children who have vomited, peed, pooed and spat. Who have stolen things, attacked the baby and shouted, 'Why can't we have a treat? I always get a treat when I go to Sam's house.' And many, many other children who have been a delight to entertain. Basically, every permutation of good, bad and indifferent playdate.

These days, I don't care as much (in a *good* way – of course I still care for the safety and happiness of children on my watch). It's just that now, I know that no matter how dreadful, it will all be over in a couple of hours. And that even the climbing-on-furniture ones aren't bad people, just a little over-excited.

But I am still astonished at how the whole thing has taken off. I mean, when did this happen?

'Maybe You Could Vacuum the Stairs?'

'I had my son when I was twenty-five, way ahead of other people I knew, and way before mothering became a sacrament for our age group, so I was spared a lot of the nonsense. I mean, what *is* a playdate?'

That's a friend of mine, mother of one teenage boy. She's pretty certain none of this existed when she was at the coal face, just thirteen years ago. It most certainly didn't exist when my mother was.

We never had playdates. Very occasionally a friend would come home from school on a Wednesday afternoon, but this could be a nerve-wracking experience, because in those days, certainly in our house, the idea that anyone would make an effort to accommodate the likes or dislikes of a visiting child would have been as unimaginable as asking the cat if it would prefer another brand of tinned food. Now, of course, we all bend over backwards, making sure the playdate child has a lovely time and isn't freaked out by anything too unfamiliar or thwarted in any way.

Back then, if the child didn't fit into family life exactly as it was – i.e. let the little ones play, be nice to them, eat whatever strange food was produced (tomato sauce with broad beans and brown rice, aubergine roasted in the oven with olive oil and oregano) and do massive amounts of 'helping' in the form of tidying up, wiping counters, carrying shopping bags and so forth – my mother was perfectly capable of refusing to have them back, even of telling them there and then that she was not very pleased by their behaviour. I still remember one friend, when I was about thirteen, asking politely, 'Is there anything I can do to help, Mrs Hourican?' in her piping English voice. She was trying to expedite the process of me leaving the house. She probably expected to pick up a few toys or flick a duster.

'How kind, Nicola. Maybe you could vacuum the stairs? And the floor needs a really *good* wash.'

Sometimes the boot went onto the other foot. I will never forget the look on the face of my friend Judy's mother when she arrived to collect her one hot summer's evening and was nearly knocked over by Judy rushing to the door and shouting, 'We went to the park and Emily's mum let us play in the fountain and my clothes got all wet but we just took them off. It was amazing, when can I come back and play again?' Nobody except the Moroccan kids played semi-naked in fountains. Certainly not nicely brought-up little Irish girls. It was years before Judy came back.

Before, there was the odd birthday party to which your child may or may not have been invited, and because these were usually in people's houses rather than anonymous adventure centres, you could easily tell yourself, 'Well, they can't invite *everyone...*'

Now, every single week brings the misery of social competitiveness: who's going where and is your child invited? And if he *isn't*, is it your fault for not keeping up? Playdates are the office parties of kid land: the stakes are higher than they seem, the waters more treacherous than they look and opting out is harder than you think.

At my children's school, every Friday at pick-up, a seething mass of kids erupts from the yard, all shouting, 'I'm going to Sean/ Sarah/Luke's house. Where are you going?' It's as much a part of the weekly calendar as tennis lessons on a Tuesday or football training on a Thursday. And the kids who aren't going anywhere that week look perfectly miserable.

We pitch these playdates as no big deal. Relaxed, fun, just a laugh. But remember that corporate law firms do the same thing with their Team-Building Away Days. Just a laugh. Ha! Everyone knows damn well that their abilities and commitment to the firm are being extrapolated from the way they react to swinging on a knotted rope across a muddy swamp or problem solve their way around an obstacle course.

For every mother who merrily chucks a gang of kids into her 4x4, feeds them pizza and juice, then whooshes them out the back garden to the trampoline or football goals, there's another who *dreads* her turn coming around.

Working mothers who have to book an afternoon off to do their bit, because their kids are usually in after-school or they think it isn't fair to ask the minder to cope with extra heads.

Mothers without a back garden who can't just 'open the doors and let them at it'. Who have to find ways to entertain them indoors or trek them up to the park and back.

Health-and-safety-conscious mothers who live in fear that something will happen to a child on their watch. Who view the normal boisterous kiddie carry-on as so many potential broken bones and cut knees. 'Whatever about my own running off or under a car, imagine if it happened to a child in your care?' I have heard this countless times. We all think it at some stage. Having charge of other people's children is a scary business, not to be undertaken too lightly.

Then there are mothers who simply loathe the inevitable mess, the noise, the playground politics brought indoors. Who count down the final half-hour to collection time: 'Just another fifteen minutes … just another five minutes…'

These aren't bad mothers. They just don't enjoy the requirements of playdates. And yet they are tyrannised by the current ubiquity of them. They feel guilty, for their children's sakes, if they don't get involved because they know their children will suffer, just a small bit.

Because for all the wonderful mothers who see that some kid isn't going anywhere and say 'I'll take him', regardless of turns, there are always a couple keeping score. No matter how informally, this tally is being run – who went where and whether the playdate was reciprocated. You might get away with one unreturned visit, but you won't get two. If you don't pay your playdate debts, your child will simply stop being invited, no matter how well liked he or she is by their peers. Because the kids don't decide, the mothers do.

Daddy Daycare

No matter how much you and I might dread playdates, spare a thought for the poor fathers who get sucked into them. I once heard a male friend, a writer who works from home and is therefore very involved in the day-to-day business of childcare, talking to another, similarly placed man about the pitfalls.

'I refuse to be the only adult in the house at pick-up time, especially if a kid has come for the first time. I've done it, and I can see the mother covertly looking around, trying to see if there is anyone else there, or if her kid has been alone with a man all afternoon.'

His companion shuddered in recognition, then story-topped: 'At least you have boys. I have a daughter. Her friends are *girls*. We didn't have playdates for the first two years because of that.'

'The worst is when they disappear off upstairs, to hide, because they don't want to go home, and you have bring them back down, *carrying* them because they're struggling so hard.'

'Oh god...' Major shudder.

I tried to tell them they were mistaken, that no one is thinking like that, but they looked pityingly at me and launched into a dissection of the subtle social ostracisation of the school gates.

'They all go for coffee after drop-off on a Friday morning, and if they do suggest I join them, I can see they hope I'll say no. Obviously, I say no.'

'*Obviously.*' With feeling.

Then they swapped tips on the Best Ways To Reassure Someone You Are Not A Paedophile In Fifteen Seconds: 'talk about sport, but never, ever say you coach a team'; 'cooking is fine, but don't be seen baking'; 'make sure they know you're working on something from home, not *just* minding children'.

You see, it's not as simple as inviting a small child to your house for a couple of hours, letting them run around and make a mess, giving them something to eat and sending them home. Perhaps nothing ever is.

In inviting that child, you are also inviting the child's parents, and you are inviting judgement – on your choice of interiors, food, toys, even garden furniture. It's low-key, almost idle judgement, but judgement all the same.

You are possibly doing violence to your own feelings – almost certainly to your house – and, most importantly, you are doing it *all the time*. Not just once a year, like a birthday, but quite possibly several times a month if you have more than one child.

It is a tyranny and an imposition. It is also here to stay. So let's set some rules around it.

Playdate Rules

Anyone who had children before 1995 is going to laugh in disbelief at the idea that playdates need rules. But trust me, they do.

Here are a couple of things to keep in mind that will make navigating the children, and their parents, easier:

- They are always psycho at first. Any small child visiting your house for the first time is likely to expect a cross between Disneyland and the panto. That's just children's imaginations. They will be over-excited and this will translate into shouting and chucking stuff around. You will wonder if there is something wrong with them – until you see your own child doing exactly the same thing. Only when they have come for a second and third time will you be able to get an idea of their character.

- Never go upstairs in someone else's house, even if your child is hiding there and refusing to come down so you can leave. Wait and allow the mother of the house to bring your LD down. We all have a right to a showhouse illusion (ish, in my case; very ish) that lasts just beyond the bend in the stairs.

- Go easy on the competiveness. It's a playdate, not a series of choreographed North Korean rallies to showcase the gloriousness of the regime. It's fine to just let them play together and then maybe watch a DVD.

- What you feed them *does* matter. It's a fine line here. Anything too outré and you will scare the visiting child and shame your own (no lentils, even shaped into 'burgers'; no weird fruit – mangoes, guava, passion fruit; definitely no stew). But stuff them full of jelly snakes, oven chips and cookies and you will be judged for being a bad and lazy mother.

- No matter how good your spaghetti Bolognese is, the child will always say their mum's is nicer. Even if their mum simply squirts a load of ketchup onto cooked mince. Don't take this personally.

- When the mother comes to collect, resist the urge to tell her how you all played Super I Spy and Junior Scrabble and had such fun, or how you 'gave them all tofu but I was so surprised that Johnny has never seen an avocado before...' She will hate you. Rightly.

- Don't tell visiting children off until they have been at least three times, or they will think you are scary and won't want to come again.

- That said, if they are monsters who throw toys at walls and push the baby down every time she tries to play, perhaps you don't really want them to come again.

- Do return playdates promptly, but really, it doesn't have to be exactly a week later. This is not a rapid response situation.

Other mothers won't think you're taking shameless advantage if you let it go a couple of weeks.

- By all means, do ask the collecting parent if they want a cup of coffee, but do not offer wine before 6pm (unless you know them *very* well).
- Now is not the time to be too casual in your verbal delivery. If you say 'oh, I just chucked them all out the back and threw a few pizzas into them', someone might believe you did just that and that their precious darling is at risk in your home.
- Don't get offended when a visiting child says 'why is your fridge so old?' or 'why does your Play-doh look like snot?' This may be simple curiosity rather than judgement. And if not, who cares? It's only a child. I have known mothers who actually cry over such comments.
- Nice kids generally have nice parents. But horrid kids can have nice parents too. Don't read too much into his home life, even if little Johnny is a total pest.
- You can't pick your child's friends, but you can decide who gets to come to your house. If little Johnny or Susie behave like total maniacs every time, you don't have to keep inviting them.
- Childhood friendships can be like relationships. Sometimes it's kinder just to end them rather than keep inviting some kid who was in Montessori with yours ten years ago.
- The good news is that once they turn eleven or twelve, they will just use the house like a hotel, calling in for food or things they've forgotten on their way to somewhere more exciting, or will sit in darkened bedrooms all afternoon playing Mass Effect on the Xbox. At which point you are welcome to go back to your life.
- If you really, really hate playdates, save up coupons for those adventure centres where they do it all for you. Take a gang of kids, turn them over to the supervisory forces and kick back in

the café till it's time to take them home. Debt paid, honour salvaged, sanity ensured.

Chapter 19

FUTURE-PROOF PARENTING

In which I discover that it's not enough to be a good parent Now

My eldest was barely a year old when, in a fit of panic, I succumbed to future-proofing.

'You really should enrol him in music class,' a friend said firmly. 'It'll stand to him later.'

She had some vague connection to make between music and maths, and general neurological development and training the inner ear. It was enough for me, so damn keen was I to give him 'the best possible start'.

So every week, I trudged up the canal, kid in buggy, icy wind in our faces, for half an hour of being patronised by a lady who could get the full gamut of scales, in ascending order of pitch, out of 'hello class'. (You should have heard what she could do with 'everybody line up').

The kid hated it. I hated it. The teacher seemed to hate us. Eventually, heavily pregnant, I decided to let us all off the hook and stopped going. Thinking back now, I can add those music lessons to a long list of 'improving' things, including:

- Story cubes (to encourage speech, comprehension and communication skills).
- Number jigsaw (to encourage early familiarity with numbers. Yawn).
- Huge, plain cardboard rocket (to encourage imaginative play through lack of bells and whistles. That went into the garden on Day Two, got wet and slowly disintegrated into a vast heap of soggy cardboard. They preferred it like that).
- Sandpit (to encourage motor-neuron skills by making castles and shapes. For six months, until time and tide did their thing, there was sand *everywhere*. Every day was like a bad summer holiday).
- Alphabet wall chart (to encourage familiarity with sounds and letters. Entirely ignored by each successive child).

I'm sure there's more that I'm forgetting, mostly because it's too painful to remember. Those things cost *money*. A lot of money, in some cases (cardboard rocket, I'm looking at you). None of them worked in promoting whatever they were supposed to promote. How can I possibly know that? Simple. No one ever played with them. Even the sandpit was a three-day wonder. The process of transferring every grain of it from pit to house was more a matter of osmosis, or wind, than of eager little hands.

My children preferred either the incredibly simple – blocks, big jigsaws, books – or incredibly complicated, stuff that sang, danced, whistled and all but landed a space pod on the moon.

Each one of those purchases was inspired by the idea of future-proofing. Even though I never heard the term until afterwards, I was very familiar with the concept: enhance their chances of future success by stockpiling Things That Do Them Good now – everything from breast milk to baby yoga.

The concept was coming at me from all angles. Because if there's one thing the Shoulderati *love*, it's the Spectre Of Future Disaster. What better stick to beat us mothers with than something dreadful that *might* happen one day because of a failure of ours now? The very nebulousness of it plays straight into their hands.

So what if they can't prove a causal link between the inadequacies of an adult life and the screw-ups of their parents? In the absence of 'is', they play fast and loose with *should*.

And so we enter the territory of risk avoidance. Now what on earth does that have to do with childhood? Surely risk avoidance belongs to a dreary world of health and safety, HACCP rules and personal injury claims? Whereas childhood is gloriously emotional, trailing clouds of glory, à la Wordsworth, full of fun and innocent mischief?

Well, maybe once upon a time the connection between the two was no more than that between childhood and, say, HGV manoeuvres. But that was before we, as a society, took up risk avoidance with such enthusiasm that it is now a basic, entry level position to our lives rather than an optional add-on.

Stop the Bus!

In the last twenty years, we have become addicted to avoiding Bad Things long before these are set to happen, even when we have no idea if these ever will happen. We plot and plan and scheme to banish all dangers and negative outcomes, no matter how remote the possibility of them occurring, far into the future.

So it's perfectly normal to eat healthily now in order to prevent cancer. To exercise in order to prevent obesity. To stash away half our wage into a pension. We are constantly planning for a perfect future, even though we have no idea if we will live to see tomorrow.

These things are motivated by the ever-increasing urgency of what we hear around us. The frantic catastrophising of the media, urging us to make ourselves safer, to risk assess every aspect of our lives and take appropriate action. Insure your house. Insure your car. Insure your health. Insure your children's mental health.

And this is fine, to a point.

On balance, we probably *will* live to see tomorrow. And the day after. Even seventy-plus years old. It's entirely sensible to take precautions to ensure this life span will all unfold in a pleasant and smooth fashion.

But when we start getting into really nebulous territory, of a time so far in the future that we can only guess at it, or a connection so casual as to be mere guesswork, then I feel the need to shout, 'Stop the bus! It's all gone a bit mad!'

I mean, it's all very well to decide to 'eat healthily', but look closer and the messages are very obscure. 'Eat oily fish, but not too much tuna because it has high levels of mercury.' 'Make sure you get enough vitamin C, but not too much because it can trigger cancer and rheumatoid arthritis.' 'Maintain a healthy body weight, but don't obsess over it because that causes stress.' 'Sleep eight hours, but oooh, be careful not to sleep more than that, because that's bad for you' and on and on and on.

We are constantly making mental calculations based on 'if' and then doing mental double-takes as a second bit of evidence comes along to contradict the first. And our calculations are getting wilder and wilder as our quest for the perfectly designed outcome gathers pace. We don't just want 'OK' or 'acceptable' anymore. We want 'exceptional', in everything from interior decorating and personal growth to CV layout.

We're also chasing this ideal future for our kids, and we're starting earlier and throwing the net wider. We select their after-school activities according to how 'useful' they will be – from learning another language, which is obviously useful, to music appreciation, which *may* help neuron alignment in the brain, but equally, it may not. Or not significantly.

But who cares, let's chuck it in the basket anyway, just in case.

Now and For Ever

Because of the obsession with risk avoidance, we have taken to assessing the things our children do, and the way we behave towards them as parents, on a weird sort of sliding scale, into which we factor everything from *Now* to *In The Future.*

In deciding whether to leave a baby to cry or respond instantly to their needs, for example, we base the decision on what's going on at that moment, but also on our understanding of the future effects of leaving a child to cry.

And we do it almost without thinking these days. This kind of impossible-to-verify future calculation goes into all our childrearing practices. We give them fruit and veg Now so that they will develop good eating habits Later. We make them tidy up their toys Now so that they learn habits of order for Later. We impose discipline on them Now so that they don't grow up spoiled Later. Encourage them Now to avoid low self-esteem Later. We praise them for specific, not general things ('you tried very hard at that and you did well', not 'you are amazing and a genius!') Now, because studies show that too much general praise actually makes them anxious and underachieving Later. And so on.

Every action is loaded with huge significance: Now and For Ever. It's like some kind of sacred vow, except we're taking it over menial stuff, like should they be allowed a biscuit before dinner or will that ruin their appetite, and – worse! – cause them to form sloppy eating habits and lead to obesity?

For the conscientious modern parent, it's not just a biscuit.

The End of History. Except It Wasn't.

I perfectly understand *why* we do all this.

We do it because child psychology is a major growth area, part and parcel of the explosion in pop psychology generally, the rise in self-help books and the belief that humanity can be perfected. We know so much more about what goes on inside children's heads (while still being substantially in the dark) and we know that the things we do as parents have huge repercussions on later outcomes. And so we are mad keen to 'get it right', whatever 'right' is.

And we do it because we know that the future is a difficult and uncertain place, in a way that our parents, happy offshoots of the 50s and 60s, didn't know. They came of age and launched their careers in a time of plenty, of upward social mobility, where full employment and financial certainty bathed everything in a lovely, secure glow.

Once they got a job, all they really had to do was be good at that job (sometimes just OK would do it) and they quite naturally progressed up the career ladder, amassing a slightly larger wage with each step, until eventually, at sixty-five, they retired to the life they deserved. Their world was quite a settled, predictable place.

OK, I'm whitewashing a little, and of course that was largely men, rather than women, who stepped so steadily. But women were married to these men and so they and their families shared in the certainties. It's not nothing.

By and large, each generation improved on the one before, becoming better educated, with better social mobility and access, and bigger dreams. In the words of the American political scientist Francis Fukuyama, it was the End Of History.

Except that it wasn't.

The good times ground to a halt somewhere around 2000 (just in time for me to get married and start thinking about a family. Thanks, guys!), and since then we have seen the world our children will inherit become more uncertain, difficult and demanding. The one thing we do know is that we don't know anything. We have no idea what shape our world will have when these children are old enough to look for jobs and forge their lives. But that isn't a very comfortable thing to admit.

And so, in a spirit of panic, we are madly trying to give them 'an edge' in any way we can. Whether it's teaching them Mandarin Chinese, CoderDojo programming technology, lateral thinking, problem solving, self-confidence, chess or even violin, part of it is with an eye to this looming difficult future, where power structures, religious dominance and ethnic balance will all be different to anything we have known.

We think that if we can equip them right, give them a little more than their peers, they will succeed in the battle for survival. In the short term, this means that we are making decisions based on crystal-ball gazing as much as any rational principle of prediction.

Maybe you think I'm insanely complacent – and you may be right – but I have so little faith in my tea leaves reading that I have decided that the best bet is to try to encourage the simple things, like mental flexibility, fundamental decency, a positive attitude and old-fashioned guts. And I think these things can be learned just as well through football, rugby, GAA, I Spy, a spot of Scrabble, DVDs of *Harry Potter*, a love of reading and endless amounts of chatting as anything especially improving. (Time, of course, will have the last word on this, and I do not at all wish to be reminded of this attitude should it turn out that I have backed quite the wrong horse.)

One result of this wild future-proofing is that we are suffering future guilt. And you don't need me to tell you how crazy that is.

Future Guilt

Here's how future guilt works in my house: Tuesday afternoon, rain bucketing down, children whinging. I'm too tired to do anything constructive with them, so I've plonked them in front of the TV. This is *bad*, because apparently it's better for their development if they do things like paint and play board games. Maybe I should take out Snakes & Ladders? But I hate Snakes & Ladders, and the littlest one will just tip the board over, which will make the others shout at her, and then I'll shout at them. But they can't just sit and watch TV all afternoon, can they?

Yes, I'm feeling guilty over an unspecified possible future lack in my children's psychology – the benefits they are not accruing because I have failed to play my part in the way I should.

How nuts is that? And anyway, what about the vague future damage caused by a mother who felt constantly guilty? Are the Shoulderati considering that? Or one who shouted at them because she didn't have the necessary patience that day to play games of skill with small children? Surely I can balance the score by appealing to the future psychological damage I spared them by taking the path of least resistance. TV for them, Jilly Cooper for me and a brief respite from the constant effort to be better.

Studies Show…

Science is naturally keen to do its bit here by conducting 'studies' that will show us the future effect of our present failings. Thanks, Science.

Try typing random words into Google – start with 'study' and then 'child development', then add, well, pretty much anything you can think of. You are bound to find a 'study' to connect them.

Studies show … children who eat breakfast do better in school.
Studies show… children who eat carrots have a lower rate of gastric ulcers and digestive disorders as adults.
Studies show… children who learn how to swim at a young age reach many developmental milestones earlier than the norm.

Studies show ... children who keep pets are healthier and more
   emotionally balanced.
Studies show ... children who live in chaotic households behave
   less well.

I'm not making any of this up. Each one of those is a verifiable
study, often widely reported in the media, who of course simply
adore them because they're a way of keeping childrearing on the
front page and giving us parents yet another stick to beat ourselves
with. ('Did you see what that study said about swimming lessons? I
knew I needed to get that sorted.')

The good news, though, is that you can probably find studies
that directly contradict each of these if you are so minded. And
that is perfectly ethical. Everybody is guilty of cherry-picking the
studies that suit their point of view and using them as a mallet to
beat the opposition with.

What the media don't often report is that these studies may
have been conducted without much in the way of scientific rigour.
I mean, I could conduct some studies right here, right now.

Studies show ... that turning off the TV and forcing my children
   to play Boggle starts with a lot of grumbling and moaning, but
   ends in general hilarity and a smug feeling for me.
Studies show ... that not feeding my children a proper lunch leads
   them to whinge and behave badly later and a guilty feeling for me.
Studies show ... the longer I spend looking for evidence of any
   crackpot theory I might have, the more likely I am to find it.

Hurray for the Studies!

Even where there is nothing much wrong with the studies
themselves, the sheer number of them is contributing hugely to
corrosive parental guilt and confusion. We wish to risk-avoid for

our children as much as possible. We are being handed endless amounts of information on how to do this, some of it utterly spurious. Result? We are drowning.

And sacrificing.

The Ultimate Sacrifice

Where avoidance of future risk and childrearing *really* come together and link arms in an unholy dance is the notion of parental sacrifice.

Society likes us to make sacrifices for our children. The image of Mother As Sacrificer is one Society is very comfortable with. 'That's what mothers *do*,' Society thinks. 'Give stuff up for their kids. It's *normal*.'

And it is normal. Of course we do. We do it every day, in a hundred small ways. We abandon our plan to stop off at the supermarket and quickly grab a couple of things we need because the kids are obviously tired and at the end of their short tethers. We change the time of a lunch appointment so that we can be at the school gates to pick them up ourselves. We cut back on our social lives to be at home with them.

We do it in big ways too throughout their lives. We don't apply for promotions we'd love because we know the extra responsibility would take us away from home more. We move house so they can be close to a good school. We scrimp on holidays so they can have the toys, clothes, gadgets and activities we think they need.

We would all merrily step into the path of a marauding bear if it ensured their safety. Of course we would. We're mothers. Parental sacrifice is Nature's Imperative, a way of ensuring the species survives. My children are welcome to my life's blood/curtailed social activities/career/holidays to North Africa. These are gifts I willingly give them.

However, there needs to be a limit to the martyrdom. Even for us Irish mothers. Otherwise we start to become simply the means to an end – a kind of parasite–host relationship in which the host (parent) is used up and discarded by the parasite (child), a rocket casing that can be comfortably shed once the child is fully launched. And our lives are worth more than that.

I would say that limit kicks in when the risk is not immediate, tangible or directly attributable. When we start getting into the territory of vague future benefits that *might* be conferred by our actions now, or vague future threats that *might* be avoided by our actions now. This is the point when we mothers can call time on sacrifice.

How much do we actually owe our children? I mean, do I owe my kids thirty years in a job I hate, for example, so that they can go to private school and do a host of after-school activities all costing €150 a pop? Do I owe them my weekends, spent behind the wheel of a car as I drop them to various sports, playdates and parties? Do I owe them years of shopping in Penneys so they can shop at Abercrombie & Fitch?

I'm not all that sure I do.

If the sacrifice is more than you can bear, then common sense dictates that it cannot be of real benefit to your child. Say it's a job that's going to take you away from home for two weeks out of every month and that this is going to make you miserable, but the reward will mean maintaining a standard of living that the kids are used to. What then? Do you grit your teeth and get your passport renewed, focusing on the end result to get you through it?

Your child suffers from asthma and you know that living in the countryside will be good for them. Do you move the family out to the middle of nowhere and try to make a life there?

What about staying in a relationship where you aren't happy, forgoing all chance of finding someone else to love and who loves you so that your children have a stable family life?

If you do violence to your feelings in order to provide something that's desirable in the short term, will they thank you? I doubt it.

Unhappy parents – those who are unfulfilled, unappreciated, frustrated – lead to unhappy kids. The complex, tangled, symbiotic relationship between parent and child makes sure of that.

In the same way that I'm not keen to try my hand at second guessing the future of the world, and therefore the most useful activities for my children to engage in, I'm not a fan of making big decisions – career and relationship decisions – based on what I think *might* be the outcome for my children.

Instead, I have decided that if I act in good faith – tease out the direct implications as far as I am able to – and make a decision based on what I know to be right today ('commuting three hours a day is going to cause me stress and eat into my free time, so I won't take that job even though the money is very good' or 'staying at home full time is going to make me feel frustrated and lonely, so I won't give up working even though my children would like me to be home more'), then we'll all do all right.

We are parents. We love our kids. We cannot be happy if they are unhappy (actively unhappy, not just disgruntled or angry because they've been thwarted). Accept each of those three things as being true, and any decision made in good faith is the 'right' one. Because there is no 'right'. Just 'right for you, now'.

It's a minefield, but you can negotiate it by refusing to get too drawn into future implications and nebulous connections. Keep it simple.

Oh, and there's another, excellent, get-out-of-martyrdom clause: whatever you do, they'll hate you anyway.

Whatever You Do, They'll Hate You Anyway

A wet Sunday afternoon with friends, earnestly discussing various schools and whether they were co-ed, offered enough in the way of music, art and drama, or if they could really be relied upon to mould the children's characters.

From behind his newspaper, my friend's father, a wise man, said, 'I wouldn't worry. Whatever you do, they'll hate you anyway.'

Harsh, but liberating.

Because he's right. If you make them play tennis every second day or practise piano for fifteen minutes every evening, they'll hate you for it. If you don't, they'll say you never gave them the chance to become aces or pros or whatever.

Beggar yourself to send them to private school, and they will turn round and tell you they were miserable because all the other kids had private jets and teased them. Send them to the local national school and they will accuse you of scuppering their chances of greatness by not getting them taught by the Jesuits or the Holy Ghost Fathers. If you go work in Saudi Arabia for ten months a year to afford all the material things they aspire to, they'll say they have grown up emotionally damaged by the lack of your presence.

This is their biological imperative – to turn on you and find in your careful, tentative, desperately hopeful managing of their early lives the source and cause of all their misery. And so, knowing that, you are free to find a happy medium, released from the notion that every second of your life must be led for them.

Having children is supposed to be a blessing, not a life sentence, so we need to start living as if there is a bit of give and take on both sides, not an endless one-way flow of anxiety, apprehension and sacrifice.

Enjoy now. Tomorrow will take care of itself.

Chapter 20

THE TRIUMPH OF THE WON'T

*In which I argue that doing nothing can be
Something too*

It was hiring time at work. Our salesperson had left (again) after just a few weeks (again), and we needed a replacement, urgently.

I was browsing CVs, trying to decode the various mission statements and bits of aspirational cant they come littered with these days, wondering why anyone would think it necessary to tell me they were classroom monitor aged seven, all while trying to stifle a sense of panic at being in a position to hire someone born in 1985 without being done for child labour.

So who to call for interview? The twenty-three-year-old media studies graduate who was head of the college debating team, runs ultimate marathons in exotic countries, has Grade Five piano, fluent Spanish, played Senior Cup hockey and was Nancy in the school production of *Oliver!*? Or the kid whose 'Other Achievements' section was cobbled together from a few volunteer summers in the local old folks' home and an interest in reading?

I summoned the first, mainly to get a look at such a phenomenal over-achiever. And then I recruited her, dazzled by the long list of extracurricular accomplishments and the brash winner's mentality.

'You won't regret this,' she said, fixing me with a steely glare, brushing aside my attempts to explain just how difficult this sales job was, how no one would return her calls or agree to take an ad, how she would need to be resilient, self-reliant, indifferent to rejection.

'I'm your woman. I love a challenge,' she intoned, a black hole of expectant optimism.

At the end of a week, she burst into tears and said she hadn't thought it would be so hard. At the end of another week, she left, reproachfully explaining to me that no one could have done that job.

Maybe she was right, but flicking through her glittering CV one more time before disposing of it, I wondered if the guy who spent his summers with the old folks might not have had more realistic expectations, and therefore the ability to pick himself up from failure. Or at least listen to me when I warned him of the difficulties he would face instead of allowing boundless positivism to swallow all before it.

'Failure Is Not an Option!'

The kind of childhood that's based on surpassing developmental milestones and racking up a wall full of trophies is increasingly proven to create insecure, over-achieving (no, that isn't a good thing) and badly adjusted adults; good on paper, hopeless everywhere else.

So who's to blame? Society, of course, for attacking parents with hysterical messages about an increasingly competitive world. Bamboozled by this, and in seeking to ensure an edge for our children, we parents are actually ruining childhood. It is in defiance of this message of fear and the compulsive drive for perfection that I am trying to follow a new mantra: Leave Them Alone.

Leave Them Alone is the antidote to a hyped-up culture that sees every idle moment of a child's life as an opportunity wasted.

Leave Them Alone parenting rejects the kind of parenting-on-steroids that's born of a panicked response to what is admittedly an increasingly scary global outlook, and is, of course, intended to be for the good of the child, but is actually misguided. Learning Hindu at some point may be a smart move, but four years of age probably isn't the optimum time to start. Likewise, appreciation of classical music is an enhancement to anyone's life, but blasting unborn babies with Mozart in order to stimulate the development of their synapses seems more desperate than dynamic (and in case you're still tempted, any benefits last for just twenty minutes – hardly worth starting up iTunes for).

There are many parents who camp up the complaints that every waking second of their weekend is spent ferrying children to a dizzying variety of aspirational extracurricular activities, but actually, they wear their 4x4 miles as a badge of pride, convinced their children's busy schedules are a sign of success. These are the ones who tell everyone at the school gates, 'Can't stop, I have to drop Susannah to her quantum physics club and Xavier has fencing,' while her children hang their heads and wish they could spend the afternoon eating burgers in the shopping centre like the bad kids.

And because they know that the spectre of pushy showbiz mom hangs over their heads, these parents have perfected a disingenuous line in evasion, claiming that it's the children who insist on joining (though the fact that their kids are always in the chess club or the book club, never any of the really appealing ones, like the stuff-yourself-with-sweets club, would seem to give the lie to this). And anyway, that's such a weak argument when surely the whole point of parenting is to make decisions for your children that are better than the decisions they would make for themselves? I mean, we don't allow them to play Skylanders for twelve hours straight on exactly that basis, so why allow them to clutter up the glorious early morning of their life with over-achievement and performance anxiety?

These parents are creating a generation of driven neurotics, unable to think for themselves; the kind of kids who grow up to shout 'Failure is not an option! The L-word is *not* in my vocabulary!' on *The Apprentice* (usually before spectacularly mismanaging a very basic task, like tying their own shoelaces).

These parents have forgotten, if they ever knew, that boredom is a great teacher. Yes, the devil makes work for idle hands, but idleness also creates the conditions for inspiration that lead to great feats of the imagination or impressive problem solving. Undoubtedly, children left alone will get into mischief, but chances are they will also get themselves out of it and learn vital survival skills along the way, whether it's how to escape from quicksand or how to give authority figures the run-around. Valuable stuff, both. And then there's the importance of sleep – the kind of good, sound, un-troubled sleep that is a child's right, without which they cannot consolidate what they learn, and which doesn't come if they are worried or under pressure to perform.

The driven parent is nothing new. Two thousand years ago, a schoolteacher named Lucius Orbilius Pupillus identified pushy parents as an occupational hazard in the classrooms of ancient Rome. Now, though, many more of us have time and money to succumb to this kind of social pressure, and enough insecurity about the future to find it seductive. But by hedging our children's every waking moment with supervised activities, we are doing them a disservice. 'Babies,' said DH Lawrence, who made a study of this kind of thing, should 'be given to stupid fat old women who can't be bothered with them ... leave the children alone. Pitch them out into the streets or the playgrounds, and take no notice of them.'

Leave Them Alone isn't just a glib way of making a virtue of laziness. There are serious, psychological reasons to back off from your children. Psychologists will talk about the reasons parents push – often with good intentions, but just as often because they're trying to relive their own childhood, even neglecting themselves in order to do so – and will emphasise the importance of occasionally just doing nothing. Where lives are too structured, leaving no time alone, or if they feel pressure to perform brilliantly, children start to show signs of stress. They need to learn to be themselves, and to be by themselves.

We know this already. We know that reaching learning milestones early is no guarantee of future academic stardom; we know that EQ (emotional intelligence) is at least as important as IQ, and that it can't be taught or encouraged by linear achievement. We know, not just because we have read the books, but because we remember the kids in school who were class leaders at eight – organised, disciplined and well taught by parents determined to further their maths/chess/problem-solving abilities – and by eighteen were barely holding their own among kids who had lumbered along at their own speed. We recall the child prodigies who went to Cambridge at sixteen, only to break down and drop out just a few years later.

We know it, but we still find ourselves utterly seduced by the idea that somehow we can help our kids to perform better, achieve more and make their mark on the world. So instead of playing The Beatles in the car, we play CDs of some irritating *Big Brother*-contestant-turned-children's-TV-presenter reading improving stories; we don't make mud pies, we make matrixes; and trips to the zoo have turned from 'look at that funny monkey' into opportunities to bone up on the breeding habits of endangered clouded leopards. And it extends in all directions. If our children throw stones, we don't clip them round the ear anymore. Instead, they get a lecture on empathy and walking a mile in someone else's shoes. It's enough to make any self-respecting kid turn into a delinquent.

Thinking back, if my parents had been inclined towards this kind of life prep, they would have had me learning Japanese. Japan, then, was the Coming Thing, the great threat to European and American power in the world. A supercharged economy that was doing everything we did, better and cheaper. A future where we all bowed low to our Japanese overlords seemed perfectly likely.

So what did they or I do about it? Nothing at all. There were kids in my class who did Japanese Studies – a mish-mash of language, culture and politics – although I doubt they learned a thing. And even if they had, what good would it do them now? (By 'good', I mean what demonstrable effect would it have on their careers; if they enjoyed it, then of course they should have got stuck in.) Because Japan then entered a crushing two-decades-long recession, and the Shoulderati began talking about China and India instead.

Hell, it's not beyond the bounds of possibility that ten years ago there were aspirational parents around the world considering teaching their kids *Irish*.

The really great thing is that as soon as you admit the possibility that doing nothing can actually constitute good parenting, you will feel a huge rush of relief.

Even the most pushy parents secretly long for permission to downsize their projected expectations a little, to throw in the towel and spend long afternoons on the sofa watching the entire *Star Wars* series or kicking a ball around the park.

Permission granted!

How to Silence Your Inner Active Parent

- DON'T panic. Seriously, they won't be deemed unemployable simply because they were never made president of the Model United Nations.
- DON'T succumb to peer parent pressure. So what if Little Susie down the road is reading Dostoyevsky at the age of six? It doesn't mean that she understands it, or that she won't be smoking weed by seventeen.
- DON'T measure your success as a parent by your children's achievements.
- DON'T project. Just because you're sorry your parents never forced you to learn tap dancing or violin doesn't mean your kids want to.
- DO chill out. Stop pushing them to read above their age group or learn Sudoku. Learn to love TV and the peace it gives you.
- DO focus on the bigger picture. It's a marathon, not a sprint.
- DO think back to your own childhood. Which gave you more lasting happiness: galumphing your way through 'Dance of the Sugar Plum Fairy' while the rest of the ballet class sniggered behind their cashmere wraps or spending hours lying on your stomach in the garden?
- DO realise that encouraging kindness, generosity and a sense of humour in children is far more important than bringing them up to be competitive, go-getting high achievers who high-five each other and make monkey noises when they succeed at something.
- DO remember that the world needs foot soldiers as well as generals. We can't all be Masters Of The Universe. There simply isn't space.

Chapter 21

HAPPILY EVER AFTER

In which I put it all together and try to make the good stuff stick

I have seen the light many times over the years. There was the day I threw away The Book and accepted that my baby was never going to conform to the enviable patterns therein. The day I understood that my second child was actually different to the first, as in, Ooh! A different child! The wonderful day I realised that the source of constant guilt I felt wasn't in fact me, but that it was coming from the outside world. The day I accepted that hey – surprise! – I was a good mother to my kids, even though we perhaps didn't look much like Society's ideal family (mainly it was a question of not enough crisp white cotton shirts over cropped khaki trousers and throwing heads back in laughter while swinging children around on sandy beaches).

But each time I have seen the light, I have lost it again, bamboozled by yet another glittering image of Mothershould. Found the light, and lost it. Found it, lost it again. And so on.

Because for every revelation I have, the Mothershould industry is producing yet more aspiration. And of course my children are growing, so different ages produce different visions of glory, chucked one after another at us, until the sudden blackout of the teenage years. Society's image of the ideal way to be with a tiny baby is different than the perfected appeal of life with toddlers, and again with school kids. For everything there is a season. And an outfit. And a magazine-friendly location.

I felt guilty every time I compared the fantasy and reality and found so little crossover. The process of reminding myself not to get sucked into this lose–lose situation is a constant one, involving lots of sharp mental notes: 'Stop being such an idiot, Emily, of course no *normal* family would gambol through fields of corn laughing like that.'

Looking back at the last tem years, I'm astonished at just how hard I was trying all the time to do it right. I was flailing wildly around, latching on to now one book/article/piece of research, now another, looking for proof that what I was doing was the correct thing or for evidence to suggest that I should be doing something else instead.

Where did I get this notion that there was one 'right' way to bring up a child? Why, from everything around me: from the media, advertising, psychology, science, baby books. Not that any of them agreed on what this 'right' way was, but they all insisted that the concept existed – a 'right' way and, of course, a 'wrong' way.

What none of them was telling me – certainly not loud enough for me to hear – was that My Way was the right way. That a calm, sensible decision based on the circumstances of my life and the personality of my baby – on everything from feeding and sleeping habits to discipline and childcare – would be the right one, for that moment, and that set-up.

And neither was any of these books or gurus telling me what I now know to be true: it will all be fine.

It will, you know. That's the real secret.

It Will All Be Fine

The baby who doesn't sleep now will eventually settle in for twelve unbroken hours. (I promise this is true. It may take three years, but it will happen.) The toddler who has tantrums so bad they look like something out of *The Omen* will be a tractable, charming child. The three-year-old who is constantly in trouble at Montessori for biting will be a considerate, sweet junior infant. The sulky, demanding nine-year-old will be a thoughtful teenager. The lumpy, unprepossessing pre-teen will be a dynamic, successful grown-up. Even the vicious, nihilistic teenager will be a pleasant, ambitious adult. You won't scar them or scare them, just as you won't drop the baby, however much you initially fear that you will.

The people who trust us to take our tiny, fragile, infinitely precious infants home from hospital are actually right – insane as their trust may seem to be the first time round. We will all measure up to the responsibility and discharge our duties not simply adequately, but well.

How do I know It Will All Be Fine? Because I have seen it, again and again. I have seen it in my own children, through the various stages of their lives so far, and in the children of my friends. I have seen it in the younger siblings of my friends and in my own younger siblings. And I've seen it in myself.

Anyone who knew the thirteen-year-old me would have predicted a life of undemanding factory work, a thirty-a-day cigarette habit and an uncouth husband in a white vest. Even my own parents were bracing themselves for something along those lines. I was surly, low achieving, boy obsessed and lazy. The future did not look bright. Now I'm not boasting that my life is utterly fabulous – of course it's not – but it isn't *that* life either.

The other reason I know this – the same reason, really, that we all know this – is because we can see the good effects on our children of the days/times when we are relaxed and ready to go wherever the flow of childrearing takes us (within reason – I don't mean heading for Smyths or McDonald's; I'm talking metaphorically here). They respond to our sense of inner peace and 'whatever'-ness, and generally behave delightfully. And if they don't, we shrug it off and don't allow it to escalate to the point where we blow a fuse and then suffer agonies of guilt afterwards.

So what do we mothers need to do to ensure this happy outcome of Fineness? Very little, actually. If we can just be ourselves, we are halfway there. Not a version of what we think we *should* be, made up of scraps of Society's finest posturing, memories of our own childhood, books we've read, friends we admire. Just ourselves. Our best selves, obviously, as much as we can. Ambitious for ourselves, honest about what's important to us, in the moment. Stop thinking ourselves forwards or backwards and enjoy now. Because this is supposed to be fun. And if it's fun, it's 'right'.

The really great thing is that if we can do these things, we will be happy. And being happy is the real secret to being a good mother.

Mainly, we need to hang onto our sense of humour. Because being a mother is funny. Even when it's infuriating, frustrating and exhausting, it's still funny. Take the Tantrum In The Supermarket. That's probably at least a nine on the scale of horrors within the average domestic routine. It usually goes something like this:

'Can I have a yoghurt?' 'No, love, not now. Wait till we get home.'

'Can I have a Milkybar?' 'No, darling, we're not buying Milkybars.'

'Well, then, a packet of jellies.' 'No, love [funny how a term of endearment can carry so much menace], we're not buying jellies.'

'Please. Ben always has jellies.' 'No.'

'You never buy me anything!' Cue hysterical screams and violent lashing out.

Sometimes they skip the negotiation stages and just go straight into the screaming and lashing out. And it's hellish. Few things in my life have made me feel as murderous as that particular scenario played out in all the various environments over the last ten years – supermarkets, toy shops, hardware stores ('Can I have a box of half-price Christmas decorations?'), chemists, even the National Gallery gift shop. That one ended with the great-grandmother of all tantrums, the four-year-old howling wracking sobs of rage and the baby grizzling while I cried too, at the impossibility of it all, and the strength of my desire to lie down and pull the covers over my head.

In mid-flow, as we were pounding homewards along the street, tears and snot everywhere, a group of Italian tourists stopped me to ask, 'Where ees Triii-nity College?' They stood, stolidly, wearing floor-length fur and comfortable loafers, while I, with tears pouring down my cheeks and a hysterical child who could barely draw breath at that stage, tried to manoeuvre the buggy past them as I explained that they just had to keep walking and they would see it. 'Thank you,' they responded, not budging. 'Can you also tell us somewhare that ees nice for lunch?'

It was funny. I just couldn't see it at the time. My outrage at the constant, relentless requests entirely dwarfed my sense of humour.

If my life were a novel, that would have been the moment of revelation. Instead, it was only the beginning of a realisation: the realisation that I had to find another way to do this, a more 'me' way. That otherwise I was going to go down, guns blazing, and take everyone with me. That was the start of thinking through the things I felt I *should* be doing, and asking just why I felt like that. It was still a far cry from a comfort zone, but it was a start. At least I was out of the war zone and looking in the right direction.

Parents, Please Attend to Your Own Masks First

If we can't even be allowed to put our children's oxygen masks on first in case of a plane emergency, how can we expect to tend to them before ourselves in matters of the mind and heart?

Doing this well starts with us; we need to mind ourselves before we can mind them. I don't mean 'me time' or a weekend pamper-ama with face masks and white towelling robes. I mean having a good look at the stuff that's getting under our skin and making us uncomfortable: the images of perfection, the impossible advice, the sneery suggestions. The shouldisms. Stare them down, see them for what they are – at best silly, at worst malicious – and then turn our faces firmly away, back to our own glorious, awkward, imperfect lives, inhabited by the glorious, awkward, imperfect darlings who are our children. Because that is where the answers lie.

Reader, you are already a hero. For doing, for daring and for always trying harder. The inspiration of that daily determination is immense. So let's not foul it up by chasing the wrong rainbows, the chimeras that disappear into ashes when we grab them or constantly stay a hand-span out of reach.

We do not need the *should* stuff. The Shouldocracy is not helpful, even when it pretends to be. It's like a friend whose cheery remarks hide a sly judgement: 'oh, white jeans; you are *brave*' or 'it's great the way you're so relaxed about your house getting untidy'. Read between the lines: 'wow, you are way too old to be wearing that' and 'you're such a slob'. The net result of heeding the Shouldocracy is to make us feel bad about ourselves.

And we are better than that. We know that now.

So, you've finished the glass of wine or cup of tea. You've finished the book and you have, I hope, not so much learned something as recognised something you already knew – the same thing that I have recognised in the writing of it. That the little voice inside us that says 'hey, I *know* how to do this – How To Be A Mother – how to love my children and mind them, if you will all just hush and let me be heard' is the key. That voice knows what it's on about. That's the voice we need to heed, picking it out of the cacophony of *should* and gradually attuning ourselves to it so that we hear it first, and the rest becomes background noise.

All the answers are already inside us, like fossils in a piece of limestone. They run right through, from surface to heart, handed down from the great-grandmothers we don't remember but whose stamp is upon us. Now we just need to read them.